Mending the Broken Land

Mending the Broken Land

SEVEN STORIES OF JESUS IN INDIAN COUNTRY

Christine Graef

CASCADE *Books* • Eugene, Oregon

MENDING THE BROKEN LAND
Seven Stories of Jesus in Indian Country

Copyright © 2014 Christine Graef. All rights reserved. Except for brief quotations in critical publications or reviews, no part of this book may be reproduced in any manner without prior written permission from the publisher. Write: Permissions, Wipf and Stock Publishers, 199 W. 8th Ave., Suite 3, Eugene, OR 97401.

Cascade Books
An Imprint of Wipf and Stock Publishers
199 W. 8th Ave., Suite 3
Eugene, OR 97401

www.wipfandstock.com

ISBN 13: 978-1-62654-427-5

Cataloging-in-Publication data:

Graef, Christine.

Mending the broken land : seven stories of Jesus in Indian country / Christine Graef.

xiv + 132 p. ; 23 cm. — Includes bibliographical references.

ISBN 13: 978-1-62654-427-5

1. Indians of North America—Northeastern States—Religion. 2. Indian mythology—Northeastern States—North America. 3. Indian mythology—Canada, Eastern—North America. I. Title.

E98.R3 G68 2014

Manufactured in the U.S.A.

Scriptures taken from the Holy Bible, New International Version®, NIV®. Copyright © 1973, 1978, 1984, 2011 by Biblica, Inc.™ Used by permission of Zondervan. All rights reserved worldwide. www.zondervan.com The "NIV" and "New International Version" are trademarks registered in the United States Patent and Trademark Office by Biblica, Inc.™

Truth and Reconciliation Commission of Canada: Interim Report
Truth and Reconciliation Commission of Canada
1500–360 Main Street
Winnipeg, Manitoba
R3C 3Z3

Website: www.trc.ca

This report is in the public domain. Anyone may, without charge or request for permission, reproduce all or part of this report.

For the Indian who stands at a distance wondering who Jesus is, hindered from approaching by the past atrocities of religion.

And the Christian whose sincere effort to reach Native communities is hindered by lack of understanding.

Chapters

List of Illustrations viii

Foreword ix

Introduction xi

1 Aiionwatha 1

2 Edge of the Woods 19

3 Hiawatha Belt 41

4 Two-Row Wampum 59

5 Women 76

6 One Bowl One Spoon 96

7 Dark and Light Creations 113

Further Reading 131

Illustrations

Illustrations done by John Kahionhes Fadden

Ben Franklin with others discuss the Circle Wampum with Haudenosaunee leaders 8
Aiionwatha's grief 20
Hiawatha Belt 42
Two-Row Wampum 60
Symbol of what crucified the Indian 83
First Grand Council 97
First Condolence 130

Foreword

Now I draw your attention to a matter. A few years ago, maybe nine, this took place.

I had a dream. In my dream I was standing by a river. As I raised my gaze and looked across the river, I saw great numbers of people walking. I could see they were in bad shape. Their necks were bent and they were looking down at the ground as they were walking. I felt so bad seeing them. It was like their spirits were on the ground.

As I was watching them, all of a sudden I felt someone put a hand on my shoulder. I could not see this man. All I could see were his fingers on my shoulder. He then spoke a few words. He said, "You must help these people."

When I woke up in the morning, right away I tried to figure out what this dream meant. For many years I wondered what this dream meant.

The day came when I realized the meaning. What caused this was that I was teaching children how our poeple's clan system came about. The story tells of a river. On both sides of the river two fires arose.

And that is where it came from, the raising of the minds. Over the years it has been this way and we still do it this way.

When we finished I thought of Indian people living in many places on this earth in all directions. Indian people who for more than 500 years have been suffering. Another kind of people with a different mind caused suffering among our people. Some they made extinct. They are no longer around.

On this day we have the opportunity to come together as one. It's what happened in my dream. All of this is what happened and I feel we are fortunate in my time. We must all work and raise each other's minds.

FOREWORD

It will be a big job for the benefit of future generations. When they walk about at that time they will be working together. This is the way it is. Indian people living in many places.

They have looked to the past and what has happened. It has burdened their minds, what happened to their ancestors. Only a small part of their direction has been forward. It is now time to turn around and look forward to the path we will make for the future generations.

This is where it will come from, that we as Indian people will unify as one.

> *Jake Swamp, Tekaronianeken (where two skies meet together) Wolf Clan, sub-chief of the Akwesasne Mohawk Nation. He has represented indigenous people at the United Nations, served as director of the Akwesasne Freedom School, and planted trees worldwide through the Trees of Peace Society. A father of seven, grandfather of twenty-three, and great-grandfather of thirteen, he also worked at the Men for Change Program in Akwesasne through the Iethi'nisten:ha Family Violence Shelter.*

Introduction

THE MADNESS OF BEING AKWESASNE

by Doug George-Kanentiio

AKWESASNE, MY HOME COMMUNITY, is the central fire, the capital of the Mohawk Nation. Ideally this means it is the place all 35,000-plus Mohawks turn to for political, spiritual, and cultural guidance. At its physical center is a 120-by-40-square-foot building, the contemporary extension of the ancient longhouse, those elongated dwellings that contained the apartments of the Iroquois and from which the self-descriptive name comes from, "rotinosionni," or those building a longhouse. More commonly the Iroquois have adopted the Seneca version, "Haudenosaunee." Also known as the Six Nations Confederacy, its member nations are the Mohawks, Oneida, Onondaga, Cayuga, Seneca, and Tuscarora, whose numbers are now approaching 100,000.

The Mohawks are the most numerous, with seven communities, most of which are in Canada. But of these the most complex, confusing, and challenging is Akwesasne. It is unique in North America as it is located at the confluence of the Grasse, Raquette, Salmon, and St. Regis Rivers, where these Adirondack-born waterways meet and are absorbed by the St. Lawrence. Akwesasne is exactly halfway between the equator and the North Pole, at the juncture of Ontario, Quebec, and New York.

For hundreds of generations Native people have benefited from Akwesasne's remarkable physical gifts, as it has the largest freshwater marshes in the northeast, with attendant wildlife. Eagles fly over the waters, as do ospreys and hawks, while great blue herons stalk along the shores, and geese, ducks, and loons scoop fish and plants from beneath the waters. Muskrats, beavers, mink, and fishers dig deep into the river banks, while deer, coyotes, raccoons, and the odd moose walk about the islands, browsing, hunting, stalking.

The region has abundance despite the intrusions of heavy industry and the growth of nearby cities and towns. Before the construction of the St. Lawrence Seaway in the 1950s, Akwesasne's waters were marked by the fast pace of the St. Lawrence across the Long Sault rapid, a long series of powerful waves dashing against massive rocks before being tamed by the islands at the eastern end of the territory that calms the flow into the wide Lake St. Francis.

From this ecological wealth the Native residents derived good health, material security, and cultural stability. Language, skills, art, music, economics, and politics came from the natural resources. For hundreds of generations the water and land provided and the people responded by forging an intimate relationship with the environment, which, by design, kept the earth fertile, the waters clean, the plants abundant, and the animals and fish healthy.

With the coming of the Europeans came massive changes. Land became a commodity, water was a product, plants were qualified by market conditions, and indigenous animals were replaced by pigs, cows, and chickens. The Mohawks resisted these intrusive species. Until the seaway, which displaced families, destroyed the traditional Mohawk economy, and compelled their children to become wage earners and taxpayers, bound to an entirely new way of living, alien in values and language to their elders.

The waters were stilled and became host to strange fish, the land was saturated with industrial pollutants, the air made heavy with the stench of acids. Not only did the environment changed, but the people also experienced radical alterations in their physical bodies. No longer lean and muscular, healthy and strong, the contemporary Mohawks expanded in size, carried toxins within their organs, died young because of cancers and infections. They became diabetic, obese, and aged prematurely.

The seaway caused the greatest, most profound and personal changes in Akwesasne Mohawk history. Yet a half century has passed since it carved its way through the territory and no compensation has been given to the people for the physical damages it has caused, or the personal, intimate pain endured by every Mohawk family displaced from their former lives.

INTRODUCTION

As a matter of consequence, the waters, having lost their former importance as sources of life, became something else, a conveyance for things that were not Mohawk but could be exploited in order to secure money in a region where the larger economy had no place for indigenous culture. The demands of the underground market for tobacco and narcotics was endless and the profits very appealing. A new generation of Mohawks saw an opportunity and took it. Smuggling across the externally imposed international border exploded as gangs of thieves sought to use Akwesasne as a conduit for their products. But this was not limited to cigarettes and weed; the trafficking in human beings became a lucrative activity for many Natives who worked with Chinese Tongs and Mafia gangs to ferry people across the waters.

Motorcycle gangs, Mafia mobsters, Asian criminal cells—they all wanted to cross that imaginary line, and with them came violence leading to death. Dozens of bodies were dumped into the waters that carried the corpses to the bottom before releasing their remains, bloated and gaseous, to float back to the surface. The eels did not care upon whose flesh they fed; Mohawk or not they fed well.

The smuggling attracted the cops and soon Akwesasne became the most heavily policed community on the planet: Royal Canadian Mounted Police, New York State Police, FBI, Canadian Border Security, US Customs, US Border Patrol, Suerete du Quebec, Ontario Provincial Police, St. Regis Tribal Police, Akwesasne Mohawk Police, Department of Homeland Security—all have their paws on the territory along with drone flyovers from the US Army at Fort Drum and stationary satellites monitoring every cellular phone call among the 13,500 Akwesasne residents. It is, according to a joint US-Canadian law enforcement statement, "ground point zero" in terms of border security, and the most porous crossing for dope, weapons, and aliens north of Mexico.

Yet somehow the residents maintain a viable, active, and distinctive culture. Every territory school teaches the Mohawk language, there is a vigorous ceremonial cycle inside the longhouse, the arts are growing, and the crafts remain remarkably intact. It is the "how" which is maddening. Why preserve a Native heritage? Why celebrate the rising of the moon? Why dance to the movements of the fish or give thanks to the deer and eagle? How can all this endure the massive assaults of electronic games and "entertainment"? What is its relevance?

INTRODUCTION

This is what Chris Graef will explain with her unique observations and her witness to the madness of Akwesasne. She will present a perspective based upon years of conversations with the Mohawk people. She will somehow make sense of this and by doing so help add to the narrative of our lives and explain to the reader, and to us, what it means to strive to be human in an era of limitations.

1

Aiíonwatha

The Lord is near to the brokenhearted and saves the crushed in spirit.

PSALM 34:18

ON A LATE SUMMER afternoon the car radio brought the voice of a pastor talking about how God calls individuals from among all nations, lands, and languages to be his people. The sun was low in the western sky, slanting rays through the trees that forest upstate New York. Deer rested in the cool shade. The trio of crow siblings born in a nest high in one of the pines glided like shadows between the trees and announced to all who could hear that they'd found a food source somewhere. A chipmunk hopped onto an ancient rock left long ago by the glaciers forming the St. Lawrence River. Out in the water a turtle peered above the surface and let the current carry him.

The pastor went on speaking. He said he thought cultural tradition should be abolished so it would not separate people. The airwaves carried his words across New York state and southern Canada, where a wealth of rivers quench the land, flowing into lakes and out to tributaries that gather into the Great Lakes, the world's largest interconnected freshwater bodies. Emptying into the St. Lawrence River, the water moves northeast to the edge of the continent and mixes with the salty ocean water. The flow of these waters has sustained the ways of unity, good mind, and health of the original people of the region, the Haudenosaune Confederacy, for the past millennia.

This time of year, Haudenosaunee people on their six reserves were bundling up medicinal plants with knowledge passed through the generations. There would be people tending the gardens, families swimming in the river, fishermen bringing in the day's catch, faithkeepers talking about the coming Green Corn Ceremony to give thanks for another year bringing a harvest. Environmental workers would be assessing the water and land that suffered a hundred Superfund cleanups in just a couple of centuries since the new arrivals from Europe.

An eagle spread his wings high on a thermal circling above the Mohawk's Akwesasne community, where the St. Lawrence surges through their reserve. His presence, recently restored, served as a reminder of the origins of their governance, the Great Law of Peace, his meaning more ancient than the systems of churches and governments across the region. The eagle perched at the top of the white pine tree that is the symbol of the Haudenosaunee's governance, showing how our God looks out over the land seeing yesterday, today, and tomorrow.

Then the pastor said he would like to see people of all colors sitting there in his congregation. But he had just said abolishing people's cultural separations is a good idea, unaware that what he was saying was that all other traditions should be abolished except his own cultural norm. His words, to a Native listener, lacked inclusion of the history that brought him to stand where he was speaking, or he would have known how a European doctrine had sent a decree across the world to bring all Native peoples into submission, take over their lands, erase their ancient knowledge, and take dominion over their children.

The doctrine, along with papal bulls and royal charters decreed in the fifteenth century, held that lands belonged to no one if they didn't belong to Christians, a claim that transferred land to political successors and continues to undercut Indian law today. A movement to repeal the policy began among the Haudenosaunee nations with a 2005 letter from an Onondaga faithkeeper, Oren Lyons, to the Vatican, gaining momentum in April 2010, when nearly two thousand representatives from indigenous people around the world gathered at the UN in New York City as the doctrine was presented for its legacy in their communities.

The Haudenosaunee white roots of peace spreading out in all directions were followed by the country's founders, the pastor's people, and even his own family, all of who found shelter under the branches of the pine here on this land. It was under this law that Europeans escaped from the unbearable religious disputes in their homelands to find freedom to serve God each in their own way.

What happened next made the North American continent the site of the greatest genocide in the history of mankind. There were 16 million Indians here at the landfall of Columbus. In 1900, in under two hundred years, there were 250,000. Whole cities, thousands of cities of Indians, whole tribes were exterminated using the systems of the church to implement removal and assimilation policies. The bonds of a once strong, healthy people and their sense of belonging to communities, clans, and extended families were broken. Hundreds of thousands of children were torn from their families: many disappeared without a trace; many died.

"By their fruits you shall know them." (Matt 7:20)

The Confederacy survived. They were once a divided people before a Law of Peace brought them into the unity of the Haudenosaunee, dwelling together in a way Jesus had taught. This constitutional form of government directed them to reach out to other nations with the precepts of the Law. The result would be a major influence in North America, affecting politics, economics, law, culture, and history.

The differing gifts among the people, knowledge of medicinal plants to support health, knowledge of the water, of the fish, of sewing, gardening, language of prayer, burial ceremonies, and stories handed down through the generations, are as diverse as a meadow of wildflowers and grasses that sustain the bees, the butterflies, and all the birds and animals that depend on them. With each plant or animal carrying the responsibility of its gift, the meadow thrives and grows in one accord for creation to continue, a harmony of scents, colors, and strengths.

"And God saw everything that he had made, and behold, it was very good." (Gen 1:31)

Long ago, more than two thousand years ago, in a land across the ocean, God gave life to the Christ (the Anointed One), birthed through the lineage of the Hebrew people. In his own language his name is Yeshua, derived from Yehoshua, meaning salvation. He came to be known as Jesus. The new religion his life fulfilled told how God's Spirit sends teachers to every generation, recognized in the way God's compassion and wisdom are promoted.

> "Knowing this first of all, that no prophecy of Scripture comes from someone's own interpretation. For no prophecy was ever produced by the will of man, but men spoke from God as they were carried along by the Holy Spirit." (2 Pet 1:20–21)

A thousand years later on the North American continent, God sent a teacher to the people in the northeast, the man who is called Skennerahawi (Peacemaker). He was born on Wyandot Indian lands in the Bay of Quinte on the north shore of Lake Ontario. The Wyandot are a part of the Iroquoian peoples and were known as the great Huron Nation, a French word meaning "wild boar" because of the men's Mohawk hairstyles.

Guided by a vision, Peacemaker stepped into his canoe and pushed off into the water that carried him across Lake Ontario into what later became New York state. He paddled into a land forested with conifers and tall hardwood trees, where rivers nourish many systems, interconnecting with tributaries across the entire land. Peacemaker followed the waters in and out of lakes that linked the people to each other, carrying messages and news about battles, spreading trade, and sharing concerns of the land. The rich soils nurtured gardens, fragrant wildflowers, bushes offering an abundance of berries, and other plentiful bounty.

At night he watched the moon wane and wax brightly above, reassuring in the dark hours as Earth returned to the light of morning. In the book of Genesis the storyteller tells about the balances in creation: "And God made two great lights; the greater light to rule the day, and the lesser light to rule the night: he made the stars also. And God set them in the firmament of heaven to give light upon the earth, and to rule over the day and over the night, and to divide the light from the darkness: and God saw that it was good."

As he entered the land Peacemaker understood that to the people here, the moon is creation's oldest grandmother, first of the female cycles that continue life, a radiance rising from the eastern sky, following the sun across the sky, assuring the capacity of new lives to regenerate in humans and in plants and animals as well. She orbits in the sky, bringing moisture to the soil and informing the people of times to come together for the ceremonies that give thanks for the continuing cycles of life.

In times long old the people of the Haudenosaunee made a covenant with each other, creation, and Creator, represented in the Four Ceremonies: Ostowa'ko:wa (the Great Feather Dance); Kane:hon (the Drum Dance); Aton:wah (the Men's Chant); and Kayentowa:nen (the Peach Stone and

Bowl Game). But the ceremonies for giving thanks had been forgotten. Peacemaker stepped from his canoe and found the people torn by war and murder that covered the region with fear and heavy hearts.

Songs were now about the dark times of war. Revenge killings and murders went on for generations. Elders among the people prayed to the Creator of Life for a solution. They listened as messengers came and prophesied change that would come. One of the men who would speak with the leaders about ways to end the fighting would be Aiionwatha. Aiionwatha is often called Hiawatha. Loosely translated, his name means He Who Combs.

Together Peacemaker and Hiawatha went down the Mohawk River to the Kanienkehaka people, who lived in villages along the river. The Algonquin called them the Mohawk because they were enemies at that time. Their own name for themselves is Kanienkehaka—People of the Place of Flint.

The Mohawk told Peacemaker, "If we let down our guard our enemies will destroy us." Peacemaker agreed to be tested so they would know that he was truly sent by the Creator. Then the Mohawk people accepted Peacemaker's vision of governance. They became the Confederacy's eastern doorkeepers, where they dwell next to morning.

After a long time (legend says five years) traveling the rivers and walking the paths to talk among all the people, Peacemaker and his words about good mind and unity brought thousands out of their dissension into an agreement to live as one family lives inside a longhouse. Their name became Haudenosaunee, derived from a new architecture, meaning The People Who Built a Longhouse.

The unity formed the powerful six-nation league, sometimes called the Iroquois Confederacy, that spanned 39,000 square miles, from the St. Lawrence River and Lake Ontario to the north, Lake Champlain and the Hudson River to the east, the Niagara River and Lake Erie to the west, and the Susquehanna and Delaware Rivers to the south. Linked from east to west, the tribes of the Iroquois Confederacy are the Mohawk, Oneida, Onondaga, Cayuga, Seneca, and later, in the 1700s, the Tuscarora.

Their oral history tells of the League being formalized on a day in late summer around noon. Corn was knee-high when the Seneca, who were divided about Peacemaker's message, agreed to be the western doorkeepers. Grandmother Moon moved in front of the sun, convincing the people the powers that guided life wanted them and their children to have this way to live. Modern archaeology would later find stone effigies of the Tree of

Peace dated to around 900 AD. Astronomy records a total eclipse of the sun over the Seneca's main village of Ganondagen at 12:48 p.m., August 18, 909, suggesting a possible date.

The Confederacy had to transform Tadodaho, the land's most menacing man. Tadodaho lived in Onondaga country, present-day Syracuse. He was a tyrant, described as having writhing snakes growing out of his head, twisted thoughts coming from the mind. Feared by everyone, Tadodaho thrived on the disunity of the people. But God's Spirit sending a vision speaks, "Have I not commanded you? Be strong and courageous. Do not be frightened, and do not be dismayed, for the Lord your God is with you wherever you go" (Josh 1:9). This is because prophets are seldom invited. And Tadodaho was transformed.

Elders gathered in the longhouse to discuss this new governance but strangers broke in, threatening and knocking them down, and the elders fled. Hiawatha returned home from the meeting to find that one of his three daughters had been murdered. At the next meeting another attack of violence scattered the elders. Hiawatha found another daughter had been murdered. Winter came and as spring thawed the frozen rivers and cleared the paths, another meeting was planned. Hiawatha's only remaining daughter, now pregnant with child, was killed when she was knocked to the ground.

These losses broke Hiawatha's mind and he wandered away from the people. Peacemaker heard about his sorrow and went out to comfort him.

Together they went to see Tadodaho, the most violent among the people.

This defines faith, the action of upholding what our God is doing. When it's the flow of a river, the people respect the direction because it is God who established the flow for all the land. When the trees struggle, there is effort to help them to fulfill their work for creation as God designed. The Spirit's intent through all creation is to reconcile our relationship with God, coming in the mercy of his compassion for all lives (Matt 11:5).

Peacemaker and Hiawatha, upholding the Great Law they believed to be the plan of Creator, tried to reason with Tadodaho, but he would not hear. His heart was hardened like ground trampled down by too many passing feet.

The people remembered an ancient song of peace. Walking out in front, the singers tried to sing it, but their fear cracked their voices, so Peacemaker and Hiawatha sang. As they sang, Tadodaho's hardened heart softened as soil with rainfall and became human. Hiawatha combed the snakes from Tadodaho's hair and his thoughts became clear. The song sung to him and the combing of his hair told him this world is not the same as the one that did those things to make him so bad.

The once-terrifying man became the Confederacy's first Tadodaho, their spiritual and political leader in a tradition that continues to govern the six nations today. Peacemaker appointed the Onondaga to be the Central Fire for the League, moderators who ratify decisions at the Grand Council meetings with all the nations. Tadodaho, feeling pleased about this, sent runners to all five nations to summon the first council.

As the first leaders of the League gathered at Onondaga Lake, Peacemaker uprooted a white pine and weapons were put down in the earth where streams of water washed over them. The pine, with its five needles clasped as one, was replanted as a symbol of the Great Way of Peace.

"I, Dekanawida, and the confederate lords, now uproot the tallest pine tree and into the depth of the earth, down into the deep underearth currents of water flowing into unknown regions, we cast all weapons of war. We bury them from sight forever and plant again the Tree."[1]

Its roots stretched in all directions. Benjamin Franklin would spend many of his days with the Haudenosaunee people to learn their form of governance, inspiring his draft of the US Constitution and the use of "We the People." German philosophers Marx and Engels would use the Great Law's blueprint as an ideology for communism. The United Nations would pattern structures after members visited to learn how their law promotes unity.

Benjamin Franklin and others learned not least from the Haudenosaunee about the Circle Wampum (see illustration, next page). In legend and history, the Circle Wampum also originates with Peacemaker's early efforts.

---

1. The Haudenosaunee Constitution from the Native North Traveling College on Cornwall Island, Akwesasne.

Chosen leaders from each of the Indian nations stand like trees in a circle, each equal in his position, their deep roots entwined holding onto each other and supporting each other, able to withstand winds and storms. Decisions would be made as a council with the voice of the people. "In the multitude of counselors there is safety" (Prov 11:14).

The Circle Wampum was woven with fifty strings symbolizing the roiane (leaders) of the nations, each joined to a circle of two entwining strands of beads representing how the law and peace are interdependent.

By bringing the people together, Peacemaker reflected Christ's words, "And if a house will be divided against itself, that house will not be able to stand" (Mark 3:25-26). Peacemaker took five arrows and bound them together, demonstrating how difficult it would be to break them if they stayed bound together. The strength of the League would be tested again and again and come to reflect a greater picture of mixed cultures whose divisiveness would cause centuries of hardship.

One of the most devastating weapons would be carried by organized religion. Across the ocean, when the twelve disciples of Jesus carried his teachings among their people, they encountered the question of what to tell other cultures. Did the message belong to them too? Should Gentiles be converted to the ancient Hebrew customs in order to be brought to knowledge of the Christ?

> The disciples met in Jerusalem and debated this. Jesus had told them, "You will be my witnesses in Jerusalem, and in all Judea and Samaria, and to the ends of the earth." (Acts 1:8)
>
> Three times God gave Peter a vision of "all kinds of four-footed animals of the earth, wild beasts, creeping things, and birds of the air" before Peter understood that "what God has cleansed you must not call common." (Acts 10:15)
>
> Soon afterward Peter met Cornelius, a Roman centurion who had been given a vision to send for Peter to come and speak with his people about Jesus. Peter said to them: "You are well aware that it is against our law for a Jew to associate with or visit a Gentile. But God has shown me that I should not call anyone impure or unclean." (Acts 10:28)
>
> "In truth I perceive that God shows no partiality. But in every nation whoever fears Him and works righteousness is accepted by Him." (Acts 10:34–35)
>
> The apostles came to understand that "as many as received him, to them he gave the right to become children of God, to those who believe in his name." (John 1:12)

It was a defining moment when they agreed that the message from Christ had nothing to do with culture. All peoples were to serve Christ with sensitivity to each other's heritage. They had come to a new place of relationship with each other. Serving a common purpose reflective of the diversity of a field of wildflowers, their separate heritages recognized with respect each culture's uniqueness, appointed by God.

Peter affirmed, "For the promise is to you and to your children, and to all who are afar off, as many as the Lord our God will call" (Acts 2:38).

This is about transformation. "But do this with gentleness and respect," Peter admonished in Acts 3:15.

When they carried Christ's teachings to the non-Hebrew people, they spoke about what all people have in common—the sufferings, grieving over losses, responsibility for good lives for their children, and a freedom from sorrows that has eluded humanity. As they shared the good news of Christ fulfilling the promise of their prophets they instructed the Gentiles to put aside certain behaviors so their spirits would be clear and there would be a healthier way to live.

"It seemed good to the Holy Spirit and to us not to burden you with anything beyond the following requirements: You are to abstain from food sacrificed to idols, from blood, from the meat of strangled animals and from sexual immorality" (Acts 15:28-29). The salvation of Jesus continued to move out into the world, speaking to the hearts of every people from every walk of life. In Europe Christianity was absorbed into the structures of their own cultural governance based on the pyramid system, with one man on top. Factions became divided, vehemently disagreeing as to how to worship God—all wanting to plant the meadow with one type of plant and erase the others. Celtic communities once governed by clans were also targeted in their home of Éire (Ireland), a word derived from the ancient Gaelic name of a matron of sovereignty. Each of their tribes too comprised their nation, each with their own identity, language, and place.

The nominal church condemned their dances, the dances carried on for generations expressing every emotion from joy to mourning. They danced in thanks to the oak tree, their symbol of the celestial tree of life. They danced in songs of prayer as millions left the country during the great hunger. The many towns around Haudenosaunee lands with Celtic names are a reminder of their arrival here seeking refuge for their families.

Waves of Europeans migrated to North America during the late eighteenth century, seeking the freedom to serve God that the North American Indians respect among each other. The first generation lived peacefully with the Native people. The Coming of the People With White Faces record belt was woven to record the relationship with purple diagonal rows of beads framing a white row, representing the Haudenosaunee holding up the non-Natives.

More people came. Wars came with the people. More land was needed and the Europeans quickly spread inland to build their societies. The Mohawk people had to leave their homes in the valley of the Mohawk River. Many went northeast to settle at the St. Lawrence River in the place called Akwesasne, meaning Land Where the Partridge Drums, a fishing camp in warmer months. It was named on a spring day when hunters heard the drumming and followed the sound to see the bird perched up on a log, throwing back his shoulders and beating the air with his wings to attract a mate. The sound echoes through the woods, a courtship like a heartbeat awakening with spring.

The newcomers hunted the bird when their tail feathers became fashionable fans in the 1600s and its white meat was served on their tables. By the 1760s the grouse were being brought into Boston, New York, and Philadelphia, with hunters bagging them by imitating the drumming on an inflated bladder to lure a jealous male or smoking them to death. Continuing in New York State even after it was outlawed, hunters constructed low brush fences, creating openings at intervals and set a wire snare at each opening that a grouse springs as it walks through, jerking it by its neck several feet off the ground.

The grouses' drumming faded as settlers' axes broke up the forest and built houses and businesses on top of Haudenosaunee sites of cities and religious centers still remembered among the people. The landscape forever changed.

Half the Akwesasne population died from outbreaks of typhoid, cholera, and smallpox during the War of 1812. More than 20,000 acres of homeland were gone after Quebec took the Dundee tract in 1882 that had been guaranteed to them. On the American side the reserve had shrunk to 14,000 acres by 1845, after the fraudulent Treaty of Buffalo Creek failed to remove them to Kansas.

Congress discontinued treaty making in 1871 when wars over land ended. Both America and Canada began devising ways to take away Native language and culture. Indian agents were appointed to settle Indians in agricultural communities, using missionaries to "civilize" them.

By 1888 Congress was appropriating more than $1 million a year to educate Indian children, about half contracted to missionaries. By 1902 there were twenty-five federally funded boarding schools across fifteen states teaching Indian children to be European.

Now confined by enforced reserves under government policies, the people became victims of a church that viewed them as dependent savages to be saved from a God who disliked the "lower classes," which they defined in terms of money and by measuring skulls. By the early 1900s the *Massena Observer*, written not far from Akwesasne, published articles lamenting that it was no longer a time for the sport of hunting down an Indian. Weekly, reports appeared of an Indian dying under a train on the railroad track. A young Mohawk man was thrown into prison for marrying a white girl. A white man caught raping an Indian woman was set free. A saloon keeper shot an Indian in the back and was set free.

The friendship of the original people was no longer needed. The 1880s Indian Affairs Commissioner John Oberly said "[the American Indian] must be imbued with the exalting egotism of American civilization so that he will say 'I' instead of 'We' and 'This is mine; instead of 'This is ours,'" during a time when science was ranking morality based on race.

The nineteenth-century Canadian government also decided that assimilating children into English Christian customs would best serve both peoples. The Indian Act and Northern Affairs Canada began funding the facilities set up by missionaries, while Roman Catholic churches, the Anglican Church of Canada, the United Church of Canada, and Presbyterian, Congregationalist, and Methodist churches provided teachers and education. Christmas was appointed to overshadow the date of winter solstice, which Native peoples around the world recognize as a time to come together with thanks, marking the covenant of promise that the circle of seasons would continue. The music of secular holidays displaced the water drums and singers in the forested hills that heard them for thousands of years. Lights and evergreens bedecked the bark houses.

All this time, all through this, leaders of the first nations brought out the treaties of promises between the countries, asking that policies of coercion be overturned.

Instead, the 1857 Act offered fifty acres to any male deemed educated, resulting in removing him from his identity with his people. Then they offered baby bonuses with the Canadian Family Allowance Act for families who did not refuse to send their children to the newly established schools.

The schools continued into the 1990s. In 1884 attendance became law for Indians sixteen years of age and younger. Children were forcibly torn from their families. Families were threatened with prison if they didn't let go of their children. Students lived at the schools, never seeing a familiar face because of the distance from their home communities. There often was no contact with any family for years. Grandmothers and grandfathers grieved. The arms of aunts and uncles, mothers and fathers, were left to ache. Three hundred children could be brought to a school in one day, confused and frightened as they were processed into the system. Those who came home for visits found brothers and sisters gone, neighboring friends vanished. Some 150,000 children of the Aboriginal, Inuit, and Metis people were taken and held at one of 132 schools across Canada. Some children were never heard from again. Thousands of students died of tuberculosis and other illnesses. Many were physically or sexually abused.

From the 1920s into the 1970s the US Congress enacted the Snyder Act to empower the Bureau of Indian Affairs to "protect the welfare" of Indian people, including forced removal of their children to be placed in foster care. The Child Welfare League of America (CWLA) and states trained workers to accomplish what would become the removal of one of every four American Indian and Alaskan Native children to non-Native foster or adoptive homes.

Those who survived were left with a lifetime of healing, belonging neither in the white world nor their Indian community.

Next came genocide from the environmental poisoning that severed the people from their dependable relationship with the land and water. The Mohawk, whose language and thoughts center on a river culture, the changing currents, the seasons that bring fish, songs, and stories that tell about their history in the places they stood, were left to mourn the loss of what had sustained their ancestors and was depended on to sustain their grandchildren.

Damming tributary waters prevented sturgeon from continuing spawning cycles. The Mohawk were ridiculed when they attempted to explain that the fish needed ladders if they were to survive. Siltation from cutting down forests and agricultural practices that left contaminants that ran off into the water and destroyed other spawning grounds, where men spent weeks living in fishing camps in the summer.

Shifts to high water levels washed away the lesser fringed gentian, elk sedge, and Ohio goldenrod where they grew along shores. Fish became loaded with mercury. The waters would bend under the weight of 186 invasive species.

But change would come.

The United Church issued their first apology to the First Nations of Canada in 1986, addressing issues related to the church's involvement in imposing European culture on the peoples. The second apology, coming in 1998, addressed the legacy of Indian Residential Schools. The Oblate Apology was made in front of about 20,000 people gathered at Lac Ste. Anne, Alberta, on July 24, 1991. Doug Crosby, then President of the Oblate Conference of Canada, spoke. "The Missionary Oblates of Mary Immaculate in Canada wish, after 150 years of being with and ministering to the native peoples of Canada, to offer an apology for certain aspects of that presence and ministry."

On December 6, 1992 Archbishop of Halifax Austin E. Burke said, "I cannot change the past. I cannot erase the damage that has been done. I can express my own sorrow, and the sorrow of your brothers and sisters in our church of Halifax for your suffering." An apology from the Anglican Church of Canada was presented on August 6, 1993 from the Primate to the National Native Convocation in Minaki, Ontario: "I have heard with admiration the stories of people and communities who have worked at healing, and I am aware of how much healing is needed. I also know that I am in need of healing, and my own people are in need of healing, and our church is in need of healing. Without that healing, we will continue the same attitudes that have done such damage in the past. I also know that healing takes a long time, both for people and for communities. I also know that it is God who heals, and that God can begin to heal when we open ourselves, our wounds, our failures, and our shame to God. I want to take one step along that path here and now."

On June 9, 1994 the Confession of the Presbyterian Church was adopted by the General Assembly. "We, the 120th General Assembly of The Presbyterian Church in Canada, seeking the guidance of the Spirit of God, and aware of our own sin and shortcomings, are called to speak to the Church we love. We do this, out of new understandings of our past[,] not out of any sense of being superior to those who have gone before us, nor out of any sense that we would have done things differently in the same context. It is with humility and in great sorrow that we come before God and our Aboriginal brothers and sisters with our confession."

On September 8, 2000, Kevin Gover, the Assistant Secretary of the Bureau of Indian Affairs (BIA) made the first acknowledgement by the United States for its role in abusing American Indian children: "This agency forbade the speaking of Indian languages, prohibited the conduct of traditional religions activities, outlawed traditional government, and made Indian people ashamed of who they were. Worst of all, the Bureau of Indian Affairs committed these acts against the children entrusted to its boarding schools, brutalizing them emotionally, psychologically, physically, and spiritually. Even in this era of self-determination, when the Bureau of Indian Affairs is at long last serving as an advocate for Indian people in an atmosphere of mutual respect, the legacy of these misdeeds haunts us. The trauma of shame, fear and anger has passed from one generation to the next, and manifests itself in the rampant alcoholism, drug abuse, and domestic violence that plague Indian Country. Many of our people live lives of unrelenting tragedy as Indian families suffer the ruin of lives by alcoholism, suicides made of shame and despair, and violent death at the hands of one another. Poverty, ignorance, and disease have been the product of this agency's work. These wrongs must be acknowledged if the healing is to begin."

In April 2001 the Child Welfare League of America (CWLA) gave a formal apology to the Native peoples for their role in supporting the BIA's Indian Adoption Project's cultural genocide. Shay Bilchik, attending the National Child Welfare Association Conference in Anchorage, Alaska, said, "The spirit in which I stand before you today, as a representative of the CWLA and as an individual, is the spirit of truth and reconciliation."

Seven residential school survivors in Akwesasne, now adults, made the trip to Ottawa to hear the Canadian government apology on June 11, 2008. Business in Parliament fell silent as Prime Minister Stephen Harper stood in the House of Commons. Above the floor hundreds of former students and church representatives listened. Television stations broadcast the event across the country as the government apologized for the atrocities against the people, their community, and their families. Harper spoke of respect changing future relationships. "For more than a century, Indian Residential Schools separated over 150,000 Aboriginal children from their families and communities. In the 1870s, the federal government, partly in order to meet its obligation to educate Aboriginal children, began to play a role in the development and administration of these schools. Two primary objectives of the Residential Schools system were to remove and isolate children from the influence of their homes, families, traditions and cultures, and to assimilate them into the dominant culture. These objectives were based on the assumption Aboriginal cultures and spiritual beliefs were inferior and unequal. Indeed, some sought, as it was infamously said, 'to kill the Indian in the child.' Today, we recognize that this policy of assimilation was wrong, has caused great harm, and has no place in our country."

In July 2003, American Indians across the country launched a lawsuit against the US government and churches for their abuse of thousands of children at Indian boarding schools, stating: "Thousands of the children were forbidden to speak their native language or otherwise maintain any of their Indian heritage. Children were routinely beaten and sexually abused. Some children died." The lawsuit, filed in the US Court of Federal Claims in Washington, accuses the government of genocide as part of its policy to assimilate Native Americans into white society.

Acknowledgement: The first tentative step toward healing. In Canada, the Indian Residential Schools Settlement Agreement set $5 billion aside for survivors, programs for their communities, and public awareness. The government began negotiating with the Anglican, Catholic, United, and Presbyterian churches in 2001 for ways to make reparations for the events, the tears. The government agreed to pay seventy percent of the settlement to students of the schools. The average payout was $25,000, with up to $275,000 for those who suffered physical or sexual abuse. The money became available in September 2007 with a cut-off date for applying four years later, September 19, 2011. Acceptance the payment meant that claimants could not sue the government in the future.

A question remains. What does healing mean when we cannot change the past? Could a payout of money and a public acknowledgement alone bring reconciliation or a truer knowledge of Jesus? The once strong and healthy communities now report 52.1 percent of their children are poor. First Nations youth are more likely to be jailed than to graduate from high school. Rates of diabetes are three to five times higher than that of the general population. Fresh fish is not affordable daily and has been replaced by boxes of processed foods. Eighty-five percent of foods on grocery store shelves are genetically altered. Communities experience high rates of unemployment, higher suicide rates, shorter life expectancies, and, for the first time, an expectancy of parents outliving their children.

Fewer than five percent of the peoples survived the genocide. The drumming grouse were placed on the endangered species list. During the past four hundred years, more than 99 species of animals and 240 plants have been presumed extinct. Thirty-three percent of all native species of plants are threatened. Half the natural ecosystems of the lower forty-eight states degraded to the point of endangerment by 1995. Wolves were erased from their Haudenosaunee territory along with carrier pigeons and wood bison. Black bears sought higher ground in the Adirondack Mountains. Only one percent of the native grasses remain, the grasses the wood bison had grazed before the developers arrived. In just a few short centuries, the land and water were broken.

The Haudenosaunee people turned to their Great Way. They'd been given a blueprint that would guide their survival as a people to solve problems that their ancestors had never seen. Peacemaker structured their lifeways to be in balance with the resources of the land. He did this by restoring the original covenant between Creator, creation, and each other. He gave the Haudenosaunee collectively nine clans, that are water, earth, and sky clans that continue through the lineage of the mother. To traditional people, there are responsibilities in this structure given by God and which must be honored.

Today 2.9 million American Indians and Alaska Natives comprise 0.9 percent of the population, projected to increase to 8.6 million in the next forty years. With a median age of thirty, there is a new generation experiencing a new relationship with non-Native Christians. Remembering the damage done by the misrepresentation of Jesus is up to us. It is our shared history.

Today many continue to come out of churches wanting to convert the Natives, unaware the people are trying to heal from the centuries of religion forced upon them. They approach not to understand the issues the people are working under and without asking what other plans the community may already have before they try to imprint their own plan. They fail to recognize that here is a people protecting the heritage of their children.

The two distinct societies in North America made treaties that allowed them to live side by side without interfering with the other. This is very difficult for churches to do without wanting to Westernize the indigenous thought or increase the numbers of their own church. Lacking understanding of the customs, ways of burials, ways of addressing elders, giving thanks for food, the ways of respect, and protocols for discarding certain items, they enthusiastically embark on a mission.

But the Native people here remember.

Like a flood coming through, uprooting trees and all the familiar plants, depositing branches and leaves from upriver, tearing away the underwater refuges of the fish, the devastations of the past rearranged everything. We look at it and we mourn. We can't restore it to exactly what it was before. The sun continues rising over each morning. Deep under the earth seeds begin to awake. Birds fly in and drop new seeds. It takes a long time before the day a new sprout emerges from the shores. If it sprouts too soon the winter comes before its roots are deep. Some seeds take years before they're ready to send their first shoots into the sunlight, a growth that needs winter to pass over it again.

The history of people choosing Jesus is not yet complete. When Jesus stood before accusers who were about to crucify him, he answered, "You would have no power over me if it were not given to you from above" (John 19:11). But there would come a new intended growth.

"On the mountain heights of Israel I will plant it; it will produce branches and bear fruit and become a splendid cedar. Birds of every kind will nest in it; they will find shelter in the shade of its branches" (Ezek 17:23). All the kinds of birds agree: we are thankful for this tree.

Jesus calls out his own from all of the world. He calls us out of despair. He calls us out of our failures. He calls his people from all heritages. John reported, "After this I looked and there before me was a great multitude that no one could count, from every nation, tribe, people and language, standing before the throne and in front of the Lamb. They were wearing white robes and were holding palm branches in their hands" (Rev 7:9).

The circle imprinted on the land by Native elders long ago with their original instructions has been layered over by generations of intermingled earth and the dust of both the ancestors and the newcomers. Across the distance of time today's circle may be askew from the original, yet there's an overlap, a space intersecting the knowledge of the first covenant with land and Creator and the knowledge of Jesus.

In this space stand a people of both cultures bringing a collective consciousness from all those who had lived before. Spokespersons of the different cultures share messages that increase the understanding of both, so that we don't leave this legacy of strife and tragedy to our descendants. "They waited for me as for showers and drank in my words as the spring rain" (Job 29:23).

2

Edge of the Woods

> Blessed be the God and Father of our Lord Jesus Christ, the Father of mercies and God of all comfort, who comforts us in all our affliction, so that we may be able to comfort those who are in any affliction, with the comfort with which we ourselves are comforted by God.
>
> 2 CORINTHIANS 1:3–4

WHEN HIAWATHA LOST HIS three daughters, grief overwhelmed him so much that he left the village and wandered alone in the woods. He'd sit silently at his camp, thinking about the loss of children and the fragility of life. People would see his fire and run and talk with him. But he didn't answer. He was too deep in grief. He went into homes where he was invited, but once there his sadness was ignored.

Legend says he came to Tully Lake, startling the ducks, who flew off of the water, lifting away his heavy grief. He saw shiny freshwater shells on the lake's bottom and picked them up. As he sat there, Hiawatha strung fifteen strings of shells and laid them across a pole. He felt this helping him. Words and phrases came to him that lifted his burden. He thought, "If I ever see anyone grieving, I'm going to give them these words to help them. I would take these shell strings in my hand and console them. The strings would become words and lift away the darkness with which they are covered. Holding these in my hand, my words would be true."

Seeing him there, Peacemaker's heart felt his grief. Drawn to the bereaved, he walked over and picked up the strings of wampum. One by one he spoke the words of condolence to Hiawatha that he'd heard Hiawatha speak. Hiawatha felt the breeze stir him. Someone understood. Job too was broken by grief so deep that when his friends came and saw him sitting on the ground, he was so unrecognizable that they wept, tore their mantles, and sprinkled dust upon their heads, as was their custom.

Job had lost everything, his family, all his possessions, and his health. When he spoke he said, "Oh that I were as in months past, as in the days when God preserved me" (Job 29:2). At first his friends were speechless, so deep was Job in the valley of his grief. Then they each tried to counsel him.

It didn't help Job. He answered, "I have heard many things like these; miserable comforters are you all. Will your long-winded speeches never end? What ails you that you keep on arguing? I also could speak like you, if you were in my place; I could make fine speeches against you and shake my head at you" (Job 16:2–4).

Job mirrored what Hiawatha would later say when Job told the counselors, "But I would strengthen you with my mouth, and the moving of my lips should assuage your grief" (Job 16:5). The attempts of his friends to get Job to rejoin life only caused Job to feel more alone. Job asks, "How long will you vex my soul, and break me in pieces with words?" (Job 19:2). He was being judged, not comforted. He could judge himself in his walk with God. "And be it indeed that I have erred, mine error remains with myself"

(Job 19:4). Sorrow kept him unreachable, in a place alone with God, wondering at the forces of life, the destruction of death, the hope of man. "My soul is weary of my life" (Job 10:1). Yet there is hope in all our tears. Job sought restoration. "For I know that my redeemer lives" (Job 19:25). God never answered why this was happening to Job. God broke his silence with speech that brought Job's thoughts to the world above the sky, above the expanse that divides us from heaven. He reconciled Job by reminding him of the sovereign Creator.

> "Where were you when I laid the earth's foundation? Tell me, if you understand. Who marked off its dimensions? Surely you know! Who stretched a measuring line across it? On what were its footings set, or who laid its cornerstone—while the morning stars sang together and all the angels shouted for joy? Who shut up the sea behind doors when it burst forth from the womb, when I made the clouds its garment and wrapped it in thick darkness, when I fixed limits for it and set its doors and bars in place, when I said, 'This far you may come and no farther; here is where your proud waves halt'? Have you ever given orders to the morning, or shown the dawn its place?" (Job 38:4-12)

This was enough for Job. God spoke again, telling Job to pray for his counselors. Hiawatha too had to forgive and return with blessing to those who had left him comfortless. Compassion moved Jesus to give disciples instructions to go and heal, ask people what they need, serve, be ready to understand, and trust God to work all situations for the good of his purpose. Consoling others established Hiawatha with a higher mission that came from his own understanding of pain. That call still stands today. Speaking to the heartbreak, the way John the Baptist stood in the wilderness and spoke to each individual, inviting them to come through the water, leave below all that was of their old life and symbolically reconnect with the living God above the water in our highest heaven. Our pasts will not be undone. What Jesus does is offer himself as the balance.

"For as in Adam all die, so in Christ all will be made alive" (1 Cor 15:22). With compassion Jesus walked to Jerusalem, "And when he drew near and saw the city, he wept over it, saying, "Would that you, even you, had known on this day the things that make for peace!" (Luke 19:41-2). In the original Greek language, this meant he saw how they were harassed and helpless, being ripped apart as if by wild animals, wounded, with no one to help them. "Jesus wept" (John 11:35). It's the shortest verse in the Bible, yet in his tears is the story of redemption and the power to destroy death, free humanity from the bondage we live our lives under, and bring gladness.

"He heals the brokenhearted and binds up their wounds" (Ps 147:3). "He will wipe away every tear from their eyes, and death shall be no more, neither shall there be mourning, nor crying, nor pain anymore, for the former things have passed away" (Rev 21:4).

Colossians 1:20 informs us, "through him God reconciled everything to himself." In a mystery we can only glimpse, Christ restored everything on earth to the one spirit of God by his blood on the cross. "All this is from God, who reconciled us to himself through Christ and gave us the ministry of reconciliation" (2 Cor 5:18).

From that time, through every generation, this ministry has continued. God reconciled Paul to himself and then gave him the purpose of pulling others out of dark places. Yet his heart always carried the painful regret of having once persecuted those who believed Jesus. He was there when young Stephen was stoned to death, possibly the one who ordered it. Paul refers to Satan sending him a messenger, an accuser who is like a stabbing in his flesh. God did not undo the wrongs when he called upon Paul. Healing does not always mean restoring a function, the way a broken wing is healed and a bird flies again. But it does require an understanding and acknowledgement of mistakes.

Weighed down by the struggles of harsh memories, our eyes can cloud and our ears stop hearing. There came a day even Elijah (My God is Yahweh) withdrew into a cave in Mount Horeb. In Elijah's day the people were acting unjustly, perversely, and selfishly. He was worn out by his people's failures and it seemed to him that he was the last one left who stood for God; he was drained from feeling his work was fruitless (1 Kgs 19). Elijah was not berated for being weak or giving up. Instead, God sent an angel to say "the journey is too much for you," nourish him with food and water, and tell him to rest.

Writing in his journal Solomon noted this continuous state in humanity. "I saw the tears of the oppressed— and they have no comforter; power was on the side of their oppressors— and they have no comforter" (Eccl 4:1). In Solomon's rendering, both oppressors and the oppressed suffered equally and both needed condolence. Hiawatha was broken under his daughters' deaths that his own action of speaking about change had brought about in retaliation. Peacemaker gave Hiawatha a new vision. Infusing his life with meaning again, Hiawatha became part of a greater purpose. He consoled Tadodaho as he himself had been consoled and because of that, a confederacy was birthed that today remains the most ancient governance on the northeast land. This was all in place long before the first Bible arrived on the shores. Hiawatha's inspiration to console is the origin of wampum in the Haudenosaunee culture. Embedded in every treaty belt and string that records their history is Hiawatha's response to restore a people to relationship with life around them, with others, and with their Creator. The wampum gave form to the Ceremony at the Edge of the Woods. The ceremony begins with a procession through the forests from a home village to another village where someone may need comforting or a meeting is to take place. Along the way, a long mournful melody is sung that intones a message of memories of ancestors who made it possible for participants to make this journey and who remind them how careful they must be not to forget their responsibility. This is the peace song that was sung to Tadodaho and is sung when a leader is consoled. The white pine, centuries old and two hundred feet tall before logging cleared the land, still grows generously across the region, reminding them they belong there. They arrive at the wood's edge.

Leaving the deep forest, they step out beneath an open sky. Beyond this field is the village where women have domain. The village is surrounded by gardens for harvests. Surrounding the gardens are fields of wildflowers and grasses that stretch to the woods. Men hunt and travel through the woods. Journeying puts their lives at risk. They are tired. They need to be greeted and refreshed before entering the village. They need to leave their weariness there, where even the wildflowers breathing scent into the air assists the natural process of restoring the body's chemical balances. The people kindle a fire to signal those in the village that they've arrived. The smoke is seen by those in the village. A group from the community is sent out to meet those at the edge. They say, "Stop here for a minute and let us refresh you. First let's say how grateful we should be that you arrived safely. Be glad we are all here. We're going to take away your problems and dust you off. Then we're going to do three things." Wampum is used. The beads being held are made from the purple and white quahog shell. Hiawatha's comfort is spoken at the Edge of the Woods Ceremony, first with a wampum given because of the tears people cry when they suffer loss. Those from the village say to the people who came through the woods, "We're going to take a moment to cry with you. We're going to take the softest deer skin and wipe tears from your eyes so you can again see the world's beauty and that we care about you." Because when hardship comes the dust of death gets in our ears too, they then say, "We'll take the softest eagle feather we can find. People talk to you and you are numb. The grief is blocking your hearing. We take the softest feather and tickle the dust out of your ears so you can understand and hear the compassion." Then they take the coolest, cleanest spring water, the lifeblood of Mother Earth, and give it to drink "because dust settles in the throat too. Refresh your life with life-giving water of our mother, the earth, so you can speak and eat again."

The ceremony addresses mind, body, and spirit. Wiping the eyes uplifts the mind in grief. The ears are cleared so the spirit within can hear. Water is for the body. They who journeyed there in turn say, "Now let us do that for you." Before they enter that path into the clearing, they have to be on the road to recovery. The path leads to the village and ultimately to the longhouse made of white pine, that symbolizes the Great Law, the spiritual center of self's journey, and the pine itself as a restorative medicine. The three aspects of the condolence establish the good mind, an aspect the Great Law echoed in the conversion of the first Tadodaho. It was the beginning of what would help comb away the twisted, snake-like thoughts. It is the lesson that we are to do this for each other. The Condolence Ceremony for raising a new roiane (They Help The Peacemaker) to fill the title of one who died uses the strings of wampum, which are passed from the clear-minded to those being consoled, and then are returned to the givers. In days long old there were runners who carried messages to the Native communities. A Haudenosaunee roiane would listen attentively if the person brought him the wampum belt or string. It's a symbol of the sincerity of the speaker, representing a promise between the two.

This practice ingrained the ways of receiving visitors. There was a long tradition in place of receiving messengers before the Europeans arrived. There were those who carried visions and stories about dreams. There were those who brought news about needs, deaths, births, and resources. This was a continent well versed in messengers. When the words of Jesus were brought in such respect, the people listened. Reciprocal conversations took place. If this relationship had taken dominance on the landscape, there would not be a legacy of distrust at the sound of Jesus' name.

There would today be no Native Christians viewed by their own people as "apples," evidence of the destruction of their heritage, being red on the outside and white on the inside. The disciples would have been at home with the Native peoples of the Americas. Jesus would have stood on the river shores and gone fishing with them, sat around the fire eating with them, shared the bounty with the community gathering for the feast. They would have had great conversations about how God's lessons are visible in the natural world. They would have agreed on the need for condolence. Then, there would have been no asking why all these things happened that were not just, not fair, questioning why God doesn't do something. There would instead be sharing how God has done something. He sent his son. The most unfair thing that ever happened was the crucifixion of his son, innocent of all wrongs. Wampum strings and belts continue to be kept today in treaties with the new countries, bringing understanding of each other, reaffirming relationship, woven to take on the concerns of each other. These contain images that are embedded in each community, made by our ancestors who were thinking of us, to be passed to the children to hold for those not yet born. As Hiawatha said, they imbue the holder to speak words that are honorable and true.

The practice continues. In summer 2007 a group of Mohawk people held an Edge of the Woods Ceremony at Mallorytown landing in the Thousand Islands National Park of Canada where there was a battle during the War of 1812, leaving many scarred and many dead. Extending their condolence to visitors they performed the ceremony, also known as Smoky Fire, as it was once done for leaders in America and Canada, reaching out and offering relationship.

Strings of wampum are used for naming ceremonies, burials, seasonal ceremonies, and communication to convene a council. Wampum has been used in lieu of a Bible in both American and Canadian courthouses. The condolence today is in response to assimilation, policies, soldiers returning from war, and loss of family. It was given to be used in the onslaught of the land that caused a loss of connection that had sustained generations. It was there to remind that God extends restoration to each generation, renewing the circle of the covenant. It reminds us, as Hiawatha established, of the need for good mind to be reciprocal.

In all of his responses, Jesus addressed the heart, not reacting to words or deeds; he looked only at the authentic within everyone. He called Peter Cephas, meaning Rock in the Syriac language.

Peter, whose behavior fell far short of standing steadfast, was revived by his great love for Jesus.

Without an understanding of the rights of freedom Jesus gave to each of us to follow our conscience, the issues that stand between the first people of the land and the churches and governments will continue to simmer. Be tenderhearted, Paul taught, remembering how we each struggle. Canada is only 145 years old. America is 237 years old. We are very young countries, yet we are the forefront of an opportunity to define a way to reconcile after religious atrocities committed against Aboriginal peoples around the world. In doing so, we learn to see ourselves and define our faith. Churches are central in lifting the shroud that covers the history of this land, a place where once there had been no prisons, no old folk homes, no alcohol or drugs. The churches can lead in a future of accountability and compassion for human rights, crossing the boundaries of governments that have left the Native people feeling there's no intent to come to agreements, that decisions have already been made once and for all.

As we become increasingly knowledgeable about each other around the globe, there's growing acceptance that we each believe Jesus as much as we are able to understand him. We understand that for some the tangible is in the form of rosary beads aiding prayer, and for others in the form of burning tobacco, a stone that holds meaning, kneeling at a pew, or lifting arms at a sunrise. It's intended to be personal. It's our heart Jesus wants to hear.

Attitudes rooted in the early European church have resulted in many a loss of God's gifts. An Indian from a church on the reserve saw members from the community at the river working on collecting samples with people from the organization Save the River. He called out to them, "Forget all that. You could be fishers of men instead." They looked at him, then turned away. The man had children and grandchildren and was well aware of the struggle the latest generations would face to survive, yet had no appreciation that here were people trying to insure clean water for future generations. At another church a Cree man stood dressed in suit and tie and testified, "I'm so glad God saved me from being Indian." To him, this meant an end to a series of traumas after being taken as a little boy to a residential school, and leaving a community that had no access to clean water and a father who became an alcoholic after losing his children to the schools and his wife to tuberculosis. But others hearing him were dismayed. One young man walked out.

Freedom of religion still guides these communities as the most personal, sovereign choice of each individual. A person born Mohawk, Oneida, Onondaga, Cayuga, Seneca, or Tuscarora is born into the longhouse. It will always welcome them and they are free to worship our Creator in whatever way their heart leads.

But on most reserves, there is this wide gap between the Natives in the church and the Natives who persevere with their heritage and the struggles they face for their people, out of sight and mind for most Americans and Canadians.

Arching over the St. Lawrence River in Akwesasne, the bridge that connects America to Canada first opened in 1958 to carry travelers 2.9 miles (4.7 km) across the river. Called the International Seaway, it is also known as the Three Nations Crossing. The Akwesasne land border crossing is the only one of Canada's 119 border crossings located in a First Nations community. The bridge crosses the Mohawk island of Kawehnoke, known as Cornwall Island. Customs was placed on the island for travelers to stop at before driving over the north span into Cornwall, Ontario. There was no consultation with the Native people when customs was placed on their land. The Eighteenth Amendment to the US Constitution went into effect on January 16, 1920, and transporting, manufacturing, or selling alcohol became illegal. Agents were given authority to confiscate other goods under the Fordney-McCumber Act of 1922. The Volstead Act, also called the US National Prohibition Act, brought a need for patrol. Officers were recruited under the Labor Appropriation Act in May 1924 and a border patrol of 450 officers was created in the United States.

The visits in lightweight canoes between homes or to sell beadwork or trade farm produce and lacrosse sticks were interrupted. Women whose livelihood depended on selling their baskets had their wares confiscated. In one lifetime it became a place of border patrol agents using weapons and the bodies of Mohawk suspects were found floating in the river shot throgh with bullets, often by their own people. The struggle has continued ever since.

The 1927 Indian Act in Canada forbade First Nations people from forming political organizations. Leaders were often jailed by the Royal Canadian Mounted Police for speaking out for tradition. Newspapers that decade reported on the selling of sewing machines to Indians at exorbitant prices, only for them to be confiscated; on Onondaga trying to get back wampum from Albany Mayor John Thacher; on paganism and resistance to becoming "civilized"; and on judges twisting deals to take lands out of the hands of Indians. Akwesasne is symptomatic of federal government's failure to open discussion with indigenous people.

Two provinces, Ontario and Quebec, and the state of New York converge in the middle of the twelve miles of river that run through Akwesasne.

Where today's elders once fished and swam freely now come patrol boats equipped with M60 machine guns or rifles, stopping and pulling over boaters and asking for identification. People are suddenly being charged for improper equipment and facing fines of $1,200 they can't pay. Young people are recruited as mules who can make $6,000 to $250,000 a week if they can avoid arrest. It is a place of alleged drug, cigarette, alcohol, weapon, and human smuggling, surrounded by an estimated twenty-five organized crime groups, a scene of arrests and seizures and continued dispute about border crossing rights.

Many lives have been lost, along with millions of dollars to government taxes, with millions more spent to bolster law enforcement. The cost includes immeasurable loss to the culture of the first people. In 1968 a delegation traveled to Ottawa and met with then-Minister of Indian Affairs Jean Chrétien. The government of Canada had decided to try to impose duties on goods the Mohawk bought to the American side of the border and the delegates sought discussion. That winter a demonstration was held at the north channel of the bridge. Traffic was blocked as the people drew attention to the promises of the Jay Treaty of 1794, which established trade between America and Britain. Article III recognizes the established systems of trade and travel among the original peoples and guarantees them continued free travel of the rivers and lakes.

Forty-nine people were jailed for demonstrating to call attention to the Jay Treaty, then released later in the day. Transport Canada's 2002 study reported that seventy percent of traffic passing through here each day is Akwesasne Mohawk people. Most of these people pass through several times a day to visit family on the other side of the water, or to go to work and school, or for visits to the Anowarako:wa (Big Turtle) Arena, community events, and ceremonies. For them there has never been a border. Family lives on both sides of the river. In Canada there have been Mohawk living in Kahnawake since 1716, in Tyendinaga since 1784, in Six Nations Reserve since 1840, and in the Wahta community since 1881.

A flood of complaints from the community informed the Mohawk Council of Akwesasne (MCA) of harassment, profiling, and severe racism by certain Canadian Border Services Agency (CBSA) customs agents. The MCA filed them with the Canadian Human Rights Commission. At the hearings, the MCA recommended creating a customs liaison. The recommendation was ignored. The files of complaints grew.

In the 2006 general election, the Conservative Party's campaign promised to equip CBSA officers with 9 mm pistols. Leadership sought a meeting with former Public Safety Minister Stockwell Day on March 3, 2008, with Prime Minister Stephen Harper on March 20, 2009, and copied notices to Peter Van Loan, who became the next Public Safety Minister. The letters were acknowledged months later but no meetings were scheduled. CBSA set June 1, 2009 as the date to arm officers at the border crossing on Akwesasne land. On May 28, the MCA traveled to Ottawa to discuss how the plan at the Cornwall Port of Entry would worsen an already tense situation. On April 30 Akwesasne Mohawk leaders from all three councils governing the community—the Mohawk Council of Chiefs, St. Regis Tribal Council and the Mohawk Council of Akwesasne—issued a unified statement against Canada's plan to arm officers on the island. In May the issue was carried to the UN's Permanent Forum on Indigenous Issues Eighth Session at the UN headquarters in New York City. A unity rally began on May 1. Mohawk from every faction occupied the area near the CBSA port of entry building. On the last day of May, leaders of the councils met to decide how to respond. It was the last hours of three years of requests for Ottawa to respect their resolution against guns on the reserve.

Returning to the site of the rally, the leaders spoke to the community about the potential for harm if the situation got out of hand. MCA Chief Larry King read a letter that had come that day from Van Loan, stating the border would remain closed until the Mohawk accepted weapons for the agents. All three councils asked that everything remain peaceful. The people stayed, even as nights dropped to forty degrees and showers of cold rain fell. But government officials advised the Mohawk were dangerous and ordered border officers off their post just before midnight June 1. The bridge was closed. The roughly 6,300 vehicles and 330 commercial trucks that used the Seaway International Bridge each day drove miles around to other ports of entry. Mohawk boat services carried people across the river every hour so they could continue their jobs. When the port was moved to Canada's shores in Cornwall and the bridge reopened, Mohawk who allegedly failed to drive all the way to the Cornwall port to check in, pay a toll, then turn and drive back to the island had their cars confiscated and had to pay the CBSA $1,000 to get their cars back.

Leaders point to the twelve-page UN Declaration on the Rights of Indigenous People, affirming the rights to self-government and asserting their distinct political, legal, economic, social, and cultural heritage. Article 19 of the declaration states:

> States shall consult and cooperate in good faith with the Indigenous peoples concerned through their own representative institutions in order to obtain their free, prior and informed consent before adopting and implementing legislative and administrative measures that may affect them.

On September 13, 2007, three decades of working for this came to fruition as the UN General Assembly voted 143 to 4 to adopt the nonbinding declaration on behalf of the world's 370 million Indigenous people. Canada, America, Australia, and New Zealand initially refused to endorse the Declaration.

In 1977 the Haudenosaunee had organized with 145 Native North and South American leaders to address the UN with concerns of the indigenous people. The Haudenosaunee succeeded in gaining recognition as a nongovernmental organization in the UN. Efforts of the original 145 attending the first visit to the UN multiplied to today's two thosand from around the world. By 1982, their efforts created the UN's Working Group on Indigenous Populations that resulted in a draft Declaration of Rights of Indigenous Populations.

It hopes to increase participation of human rights institutions. MCA Grand Chief Tim Thompson, attending the National Day of Reconciliation held on June 11, 2009 in Victoria Island, Ottawa, described incidents of harassment escalating over many years and asked for support on the border issue. The day marked one year after the Prime Minister's apology for the government's part in Indian Residential Schools. There had still been no agreement by the Prime Minister's office to meet with the Mohawk Council. No one from the reserve's churches was seen standing with the community or expressing concern for the leadership. Still the only purpose seems to be "convert and take them away from the tradition." Conversion to faith often comes with taking on Western values in the confusion of denying heritage.

The disciples grappled with this same question when non-Hebrews were left not knowing how or where to worship. They would no longer worship false ways, and yet they didn't belong in synagogues either. Galatians were being told they had to be circumcised and accept a different ethnicity to participate in the faith in Christ. An irate Paul said to them, "I would like to learn just one thing from you: Did you receive the Spirit by the works of the law, or by believing what you heard?" (Gal 3:2). It comes from the cry of the heart. Paul was saying that we are already one body. Healing is already accomplished. Jesus finished it and extended the ancient covenant to the rest of the world. What we're doing, like the disciples before us, is trying to understand what this should look like in our interactions. A number of Christians wanting to reach reservations hold attitudes of liking the "poor, needy" Indians when they're perceived to be without power of their own, and we feel great about our charity. We box up clothing and appliances for them, take up collections, and feel we've served. Or the words of a sermon may be good and the message needed, but the voice of a preacher sounds aggressive and loud to a people whose tradition delivers prayer in soft-spoken words and whose culture finds the gesture of a pointing finger offensive. Many missionaries even today arrive thinking they are the ones who carry knowledge. They don't notice the grandmother looking out her window watching her grandchildren play in her son's house, next to hers. Family is core. Heritage nurtures family. These missionaries overlook understanding that Jesus as a man belonged to a tribe and knew full well the suffering caused when his people's land was taken. We've been given a wealth of Bible stories in which to seek a connecting point, such as the riders on horseback coming with Jesus when he returns, meaningful to the nations of the West whose lives and battles are tied intricately to their horses.

The Americanization of Jesus that came with government policies and corporate power appeared to bring about the thinking that Jesus died for everyone to have the American dream, resulting in taking more than we need, amassing wealth in pursuit of materialism, bigger houses, and more greed rationalized as prayer for blessing. Westernized thought leapt to the victories given in the power of the cross, overlooking words of suffering, of being poor in spirit, of sacrifice, words that believers in other countries are dying for, persecuted and hungry. An image remains of a "god" who is counterintuitive to the world view of living closely with the Creator as caretakers of a land intended for the next generations. Solomon, a wealthy man, king over all the people of Israel, accumulated vast riches, constructed projects growing vineyards, gardens and parks, building reservoirs for trees to flourish. "I denied myself nothing my eyes desired; I refused my heart no pleasure. My heart took delight in all my labor, and this was the reward for all my toil. Yet when I surveyed all that my hands had done and what I had toiled to achieve, everything was meaningless, a chasing after the wind; nothing was gained under the sun" (Eccl 2:10–11).

Wise in human nature, he tells us, "Whoever loves money never has enough; whoever loves wealth is never satisfied with their income. This too is meaningless. As goods increase, so do those who consume them. And what benefit are they to the owners except to feast their eyes on them?" (Eccl 5:10-11). Done in by the tedium that man works under, he concludes with, "Fear God and keep his commandments, for this is the duty of all mankind" (Eccl 12:13). When he spoke with people, the apostle Paul centered his message on reconciling to God to enable us to reconcile to each other. "Let all bitterness and wrath and anger and clamor and slander be put away from you, along with all malice. And be kind to one another, tender-hearted, forgiving each other, just as God in Christ also has forgiven you" (Eph 4:31-32).

After Hiawatha's daughters were killed, he had to return with Peacemaker to complete the mission of bringing the people into the Confederacy. It was Tadodaho who sent men to break up Hiawatha's peace councils and to murder his daughters and grandchild. Tadodaho boasted among the people about having the kind of power that destroys. Hiawatha spoke his words of condolence to him.

In the undercurrents of these stories is the acceptance that we ourselves have also made mistakes and know how it is to suffer in need of forgiveness and be restored to relationship. "My comfort in my suffering is this: Your promise preserves my life" (Ps 119:50).

Peacemaker advised the leaders to carry no anger and to wear seven layers of thick skin so that others' opinions and the gossip in communities did not cause them to forget their good minds. "Do not think of yourselves, but act to serve others, and to be in harmony with one another," he said. This is reflective of the instruction, "Do nothing out of selfish ambition or vain conceit, but in humility consider others better than yourselves" (Phil 2:3). "For where you have envy and selfish ambition, there you find disorder and every evil practice" (Jas 3:15-17).

Top-down decisions haven't worked for healing. And we know the courts don't resolve this issue. On March 11, 2005 the Onondaga community filed a federal land rights action asking that they have a voice in policy decisions affecting the ecosystem of their lands, expanded grave site protections, and rights to hunt, fish, and gather. It petitioned the federal court to recognize treaties with the United States. This was the first American Indian land claim to be based on cleaning up the environment.

The first paragraph reads: "The Onondaga People wish to bring about a healing between themselves and all others who live in this region that has been the homeland of the Onondaga Nation since the dawn of time." After years of deliberation, the nation took steps to begin networking partnerships with local schools and environmental groups with common concerns. One partnership began with a group of people who got together and sat on the floor of a living room in Syracuse. They saw anti-Indian signs to the west saying "No Sovereignty." To the east there were death threats to American Indians and racist rhetoric. The group determined to bring more understanding to people and formed Neighbors of the Onondaga Nation (NOON), a grassroots committee of the Syracuse Peace Council, today numbering about fifteen people. Their threads had already begun weaving relationships with the nation, including delivery of a baby by an Onondaga midwife, work with the Onondaga youth on environmental projects, lacrosse teams composed of children from all communities, and participation in the Syracuse Choir.

Native youth addressing reconciliation circles stress the need for non-Natives to become educated about history and the diversity among the Native communities across the continent. They talk of culture shock experienced when a reservation youth leaves family and community to attend college and the need for support in academic institutions. They want their language and heritage and for policies to separate independent powers as well as a way to work together on concerns of both Native and non-Native peoples. During the reconciliation talks many elders said "it is the white people who need to find a way to heal." They are the ones who need to be reached with compassion, have their eyes cleared. Uprooted and restless, they haven't the deep sense of ancestry that leads back to the beginning of the land. They have a far greater healing to work through as they gain historical awareness not only of the genocide and slavery that built their country, but of the use of Christ to legitimize these policies. Those who break a covenant are viewed as unaware of their need for healing.

In 1992 the Indigenous Law Institute began a global campaign to call upon Pope John Paul II to formally revoke the *Inter Caetera* papal bull of 1493. Stephen Newcomb, Shawnee/Lenape, Director of the Indigenous Law Institute, states that while acknowledgment of past wrongs is good, the concept of reconciliation assumes there was once a friendship with the government or churches. The very elements needed for healing, a diagnosis of the source of the problem, are not there to bring about conciliation.

For Newcomb, the process of recovery and a sovereign spiritual life must include restoration of language and life based on a healthy environment. Traditions thousands of years old, a part of each people's culture, are in place for historic grieving. In earlier centuries, elements of the Edge of the Woods Ceremony were performed at the signing of treaties, as leaders met to clear minds of all disquiet before they proceeded into the day's business. But when the Revolution ended the British granted the United States sovereignty over lands south of Canada, north of Florida, and east of the Mississippi, lands belonging to Native nations, all without consulting the nations.

The written word became distrusted as treaties turned out to be lies and history books began portraying Indian people wrongly. Oral history that had come down through the generations continues as time honored, trusted to pass along to youth so they too will be gathered to their fathers with honor. In 2 Corinthians 2, Paul beseeched the people not to punish an offender, but to welcome him back because not only did the exclusion hurt the offender, it left a wound in the whole group. He understood the difficulty, having himself once been in the wrong. In verse five, he says, "If anyone has caused grief he has not so much grieved me as he has grieved all of you." When a mind-set of blame is held too long it's a gateway for all the other incidents to follow that will divide a group. Paul tells the Corinthians their admonishment was enough for a man who had done wrong and to now enfold him with comfort so that he will not be overwhelmed by sorrow. He is to be encouraged.

In 1992 as the church apologies were coming forth, Canada appointed a Royal Commission on Aboriginal Peoples. They traveled extensively for nearly two years, holding hearings in Aboriginal communities and interviewing more thana thousand groups. Then they listened to others, among them the four historic mission churches—the Anglican, Roman Catholic, Presbyterian, and United churches. Compiled in a report called *Toward Reconciliation: Overview of the Fourth Round*, published in April 1994, the summaries of church leaders spoke of wanting to participate in the healing process. They advocated sharing support for education, health, housing, and environmental issues and for local congregations to become more aware of past and present issues. Listening to Native people tell their stories was identified as an important beginning in dispelling religion's tendency toward denial. The Aboriginal Rights Coalition, representing most of the major Canadian churches, advocates for Native people to determine themselves what their communities need.

"Great is your faith," Jesus said to the Canaanite woman who sought Jesus to heal her daughter. She called him Son of David, and he answered, saying he was sent to the lost sheep of Israel (Matt 15:21–28). The woman did not talk of equal rights or cultural equality. Her cry came from her heart on behalf of her afflicted daughter. Jesus heard. In John 4 a woman meeting Jesus at a well calls him a Jew and herself a Samaritan woman. She is acknowledging heritage. Jesus invites her, "Whoever drinks the water I give them will never thirst. Indeed, the water I give them will become in them a spring of water welling up to eternal life" (John 4:14). Through these encounters the people learned from each other how our perseverance for the living water would bring about God's larger plan.

In the first decade of the twenty-first century Christ sent messengers that would cause his church to correct their thinking. Indigenous delegates from around the world contacted the Vatican about papal bulls and doctrines. Bishop Francis X. DiLorenzo, Diocese of Honolulu, and Tony Castanha, Project Director for the Matsunaga Institute for Peace, wrote a letter requesting audience with Pope John Paul II. In October 2000 a delegation traveled to Italy and met with the Vatican Council for Peace and Justice. In 2003 the seventh annual burning of the papal bull took place in Honolulu. In May 2005 people gathered at the United Nations Church Center during the UN Permanent Forum on Indigenous Issues and a letter was written to Pope Benedict XVI requesting he formally revoke the 1493 *Inter Caetera* bull. Steven Newcomb received a response from Archbishop Celestino Migliore stating that "taken from the context of the political climate at the time, the notion of international law and the geographical notions then extant, the bull *Inter Caetera*, like other documents of that era, has become ipso facto obsolete and with no effect." Oren Lyons received a letter from Archbishop Migliore saying that in the view of the Holy See, the papal bull *Inter Caetera* has been abrogated a number of times in a number of different ways.

The Doctrine of Discovery was an imperialistic doctrine used to justify invading lands in the name of religion. As popes took up seats in Rome, accumulating vast amounts of wealth and artifacts from peoples around the world, they established a perspective that non-Christians were less than human. Pope Nichols V in 1452 directed King Alfonso V to "capture, vanquish and subdue the Saracens, pagans and other enemies," to "put them into perpetual slavery," and "to take all their possessions and property."

Encased in this thought system, they carried it out like warfare forty years later when Columbus sailed across the ocean. Along the way to the Americas, Columbus and his men committed horrific acts of genocide against the Native people of the Caribbean, sanctioned by the doctrine.

Columbus made a second journey to the New World to bring priests carrying a method the Romans used to divide and conquer. It has been used in the courts right up to today to convert land into European hands, citing the Christian law of nations that holds Christian nations have a divine right to claim authority.

In the Old Testament prosperity was linked to land. There were vast acres that grew produce for the people and sustenance for the herds. God gave Abraham land to preserve his seed into the future (Gen 12:7). The term "heal the land" is used frequently when God speaks of our well-being. Fundamental to what indigenous people around the world identify for healing relationship is the land that supports health, culture, and relationship to God, a conclusion echoed in Canada's 1996 Royal Commission on Aboriginal Peoples: "Without adequate lands and resources, Aboriginal nations . . . will be pushed to the edge of economic, cultural and political extinction."

Culture is a complexity of dynamics trusted to keep the next generation healthy. The sound of the river runs through the veins of great-grandparents to little children. The familiar rhythms of flowers and daylight animals retreating at sunset, respecting the time for night workers of creation—all are contained in the word for earth, Yethi'nihstenha Onhwentsya eo (She To Us Mother Provides Our Needs). This is unchanged.

Over the night is light that began from stars birthed before dinosaurs walked and a feather may have been five feet long. Starlight affirms to each generation the feeling that we belong. We are not alone. A greater story, a vastness of time, a place for those who went before us, making us wonder what would they wish for us to know, to do, and continues to tell the time of ancient solstices—the turning of seasons cradled in the stars.

The moon continues to tell of ancient solstices, the turning of seasons. The stars bring water, connecting to the land tons of water falling from meteorites dissipating over the earth, ancient knowledge of the people, knowing the stars bring morning dew.

Psalm 147:4 tells us, "He determines the number of the stars and calls them each by name." The North Star (the star which never moves) and the morning star, Venus (she brings the day). "When I consider your heavens, the work of your fingers, the moon and the stars, which you have ordained" (Ps 8:3) reminds us of principles by which to live, carefully observed cycles for times of planting and harvesting, times when fish will be abundant, when deer carry young and shouldn't be hunted, and times to give thanks. These are intricately designed lights moving across the sky to help each generation know there is a covenant. The Pleiades (Flock of Doves) is known as "The Dancers, the Seven Children" in Haudenosaunee lands, a luminous cluster of hot blue that formed overhead a hundred million years ago. It's one of the nearest constellations to earth, rising near dawn in spring and setting in the dawn of autumn to announce times of harvest. It's one of only four constellations talked about in the Bible and this one, for reasons we don't yet know, is called "sweet." The Scriptures instruct in Amos 5:8, "Can you bind the sweet influences of Pleiades, or loose the bands of Orion?" 1 Corinthians 15:41 advises, "Seek him that makes the seven stars and Orion, and turns the shadow of death into the morning, and makes the day dark with night: that calls for the waters." There comes from every part of earth a voice of thanks for these designs. We enter God's presence through giving thanks. "Enter his gates with thanksgiving and his courts with praise; give thanks to him and praise his name. For the Lord is good and his love endures forever; his faithfulness continues through all generations" (Ps 100:4-5).

The Thanksgiving Address, Ohén:ton ka rih wa téh kwen (Words that Come Before All Else), was the Haudenosaunee's first instruction from the Creator. The words are spoken by an elder acknowledging thankfulness that we all arrived safely for the ceremony. The words alight gently to the earth, thanking mother for providing all we need, and acknowledging the waters because water is life; the fish who cleanse water, and give themselves to us as food; the plants that sustain many lives and provide medicines to help us; all the animals who, having been created before us, teach us many things; the trees for all they do as helpers in creation; the birds, the four winds, the thunders that bring rains to renew life; the sun that continues to rise each day; the moon that guides the tides and cycles of birth; the stars lighting the sky; the teachers among us who help us understand how to live well; and the Creator, the Great Mystery that has provided all creation with sustenance and health, with beauty and each other.

This is spoken at the opening of every gathering to bring minds together and it is spoken at the end of every meeting so that no matter what the disagreements or obstacles faced, thoughts will be brought back to agreeing that these things are important to all of us. It often closes with, "Éhtho niiohtónha'k ne onkwa'nikón:ra"—now our minds are one. The address has been printed in several languages around the world to promote the practice of giving thanks.

Old Testament stories speak importantly about our relationship in the covenant. Rainfall, crops, and survival depended on the people's covenant prayers to God and for each other in unity. As churches started to be built across the world, dividing into today's 41,000 denominations, focus was put on the kingdom of heaven, disconnecting people from their relationships with land and water. But God never changed his mind about the original relationship we are to dwell in while living out our purposes as we wait for his return.

The book of worship in the Bible, the Psalms, reveals that all God's creations are in relationship with God. All God's creatures praise him. "Let the heavens rejoice, let the earth be glad, let the sea resound, and all that is in it; let the fields be jubilant, and everything in them. Then all the trees of the forest will sing for joy; they will sing before the Lord" (Ps 96:11–12).

The Jews too were familiar with perceiving the presence of God through nature. "The crash of your thunder was in the whirlwind, your lightnings lighted up the world; the earth trembled and quaked" (Ps 77:18). The waters parted as Israel escaped Egypt, the cloud and fire led them through the wilderness, and there was thunder on the mountaintop when God spoke with Moses. The sky darkened when Jesus died. The biblical people knew all this as God's presence. The Hebrew people also understood the importance of burials in much the way North America's people hold the importance of the bones of their ancestors, stolen to be kept in museums. When Joseph died in Egypt he asked that his bones be carried to the homeland for burial. The people promised. Three hundred years later the people had not forgotten and he was moved. Praise was centered in Jerusalem, in the courts of God's house (Ps 116:18–19). The singing people of Yahweh called on all nations to praise the Lord of the whole earth, whose salvation was seen in Zion (Ps 98:3–4), not so that others would become like them, but because all belonged to God and in that relationship they maintain peace with each other.

The churches tried to take the Native people away from this, which had brought thousands of their ancestors into peaceful governance, in exchange for what was perceived as God even they could not agree about it.

Paul tells the people in Acts 14:16, "In the past, he has let all nations go their own way. Yet he has not left himself without testimony. He has shown kindness by giving you rain from heaven and crops in their seasons. He provides you with plenty of food and fills your hearts with joy."

All peoples of the world, all animals, birds, and all living beings are sustained through relationship with water and land. When we forget, we become like the serpent of old, consuming everything.

"Is it not enough for you to feed on the good pasture? Must you also trample the rest of your pasture with your feet? Is it not enough for you to drink clear water? Must you also muddy the rest with your feet?" (Ezek 34:18)

The Haudenosaunee constitution instructs their nations to keep the council fire burning. As with Hebrew law, the Great Law provided that "the rites and festivals of each nation shall remain undisturbed and shall continue as before because they were given by the people of old times as useful and necessary for the good of men." Preserved in Wampum Chronicles in Akwesasne, petitions of the ancestors stated:

> "But we do not wish to hold of what is not belonging to us," Mohawk roiane wrote to the Queen on June 21, 1892. "We do not believe that it is calculated to promote our welfare. We all know that all nations adhere to their own form of Government and of their systematic constitutions."

The New York State Indian Commission, chaired by Edward A. Everett, presented a 399-page report in 1922 concluding that lands in New York had been stolen from the Haudenosaunee. Developers continued across the state, allowing others to move onto the lands. Then, two years after the Everett Report, the American government passed legislation declaring all American Indians to be US citizens. In response, early in the summer of 1925, the League carried eight wampum belts out of the longhouse at Onondaga for the first time since George Washington saw them, to remind all of the agreement of their relationship with the Europeans. They did not accept the citizenship.

Few of the early arrivals had interest in the natural world until the economic assets began disappearing. Hunting soon unfolded into outings to understand behavior and physiology of the natural world, discovering the value of the wood's edge to the grouse. Foresters at the time still thought that planting a block of one kind of tree would increase numbers of wildlife. Today the edge of the woods is better understood. Its meadows are an ecotone, an overlap of greater resources where a diversity grows without one plant dominating the other. There are medicines to help restore our well-being. Each has its own job, each differing from the other. Each strengthened by another.

New textures and colors joined Haudenosaunee lands in an exchange that began when the first ship from Europe emptied on the shores with the first invasive species. These included St. John's wort from Europe, soothing nerves and stress, and plantain, called "white man's foot" in Indian language because of how it sticks to the feet of cattle and people as they walk over the earth, to spread it everywhere. Bruised leaves were sometimes used as a poultice. They became an important food for caterpillars of some species and many species of butterflies. Red clover was introduced and found to relax nerves and aid treatment of tumors and skin problems. The scruffy brown burdock was brought to the US by early French and English colonists. By the 1600s it grew along woods' edges and was used to reduce joint swelling, cleanse the blood, and as a food high in minerals and vitamins. The purple flowers of the chicory sprouted on the land on high stems after Thomas Jefferson brought it in 1774 for its roots to be used as an herbal coffee.

Knowing that God's decree creates plants offering medicines to help the people, the Haudenosaunee began asking if these new plants might contain medicinal properties to treat the new diseases that arrived in their communities. Like Daniel in the Bible picking up what would increase his learning from the culture dominating the Israelites, they learned to read, organize education, understand the legal systems of the new countries, and incorporate what was useful, but not to change who they were, which would have been akin to selling your mother, your ancestry. The axe and plow had at first brought benefits of more woods' edges for the grouse and all that depend on the wildflowers. But when the tools went too far, the birds, animals, and pollinating insects began disappearing too. There was not a balance. We now know the plants' and animals' uncertain hold on the future is up to us all.

3

Hiawatha Belt

He is before all things, and in him all things hold together.
COLOSSIANS 1:17

"I SAW THE GLORY of the God of Israel coming from the east. His voice was like the roar of rushing waters, and the land was radiant with his glory" (Ezek 43:2). "And I heard a sound from heaven like the roar of rushing waters and like a loud peal of thunder" (Rev 14:2). "His feet were like bronze glowing in a furnace, and his voice was like the sound of rushing waters" (Rev 1:15). The Bible speaks of water more than seven hundred times, comparing it to the spirit of God, nourishing our strength, replenishing us if we're in drought, containing the very life of the covenant promise with earth and all her inhabitants.

> You gave abundant showers, O God; you refreshed your weary inheritance. (Ps 68:9)

> You care for the land and water it; you enrich it abundantly, The streams of God are filled with water, to provide the people with grain, for so you have ordained it. You drench its furrows and level its ridges, you soften it with showers and bless its crops. You crown the year with your bounty, and your carts overflow with abundance. The meadows are covered with flocks and the valleys are mantled with grain; they shout for joy and sing. (Ps 65:9–13)

> But let justice roll on like a river, righteousness like a never-failing stream. (Amos 5:24)

MENDING THE BROKEN LAND

With joy you will draw water from the wells of salvation. (Isa 12:2)

In the Haudenosaunee creation story the peopling of earth began with Atsi'tsiaka:ion (Matured Flower) falling from the sky world when earth was covered with water. She is called Sky Woman. To help her, earth was brought up from beneath the water through the efforts of the water animals such as the muskrat. All life comes from water. All life is drawn to water.

Christian Scripture tells of founding earth upon the seas, like a turtle holding back the water that the Mohawk tell of when explaining why North America is called Turtle Island. "And yet his work has been finished since the creation of the world. For somewhere he has spoken about the seventh day in these words: And on the seventh day God rested from all his work" (Heb 4:3–5). All the elements that would become the wetlands, the streams, and hosts of living creatures, all our names and historic moments, all deserts and sandstorms, mountains and forests, earthquakes, rock slides, and rain bursts, and the birthing and dying of stars were set into motion to move as one living organism into today, toward tomorrow.

These dynamics led to glaciers melting into trails of water that flow together, becoming places of trade, communication, travel, and ideas. Across the ocean the apostles too met with others at the confluence of waters, along trade routes that joined lands and communities. Their message was carried far and wide from these places. Water unites.

A wampum called the Hiawatha Belt was woven to symbolize the League of Five Nations. The squares of the belt represent each nation with white beads connecting the squares and the ends of both sides left open for others who might join. These connecting white beads illustrate the rivers and paths that join the nations.

In the days when earth was not dug into deeper than planting seeds or burying the dead, Mohawk territory was more than eleven million acres—17,200 square miles—from the St. Lawrence River to the west branch of the Delaware, east to Lake Champlain, west to the West Canada and Unadilla Creeks that led to the Oneida people. Epidemics of disease would flow up these rivers with the Bibles, killing thousands of people. Jesuits paddled in on canoes, believing the Native people must first be assimilated into European civilization before they could become the Lord's. Farther up the rivers in the Huron settlements the Jesuits divided the communities, weakening them until they couldn't stand against the wars surrounding them. Today they are small bands of Wyondat. The people lost their Mohawk Valley homeland. They traveled northeast to Akwesasne at the forty-fifth parallel. They built a community and moved the katsista, the fire of the Mohawk Nation. Located at the confluence of the Grasse, Racquette, St. Regis, Salmon, and St. Lawrence Rivers, Akwesasne is a place where white trillium blooms in wetlands with communities of wild mint, cardinal flowers, and milkweed. Wild onions take root in the shade, the red cupped flowers of wine-cup in rocky ground. An inquisitive blue heron folds its legs and takes graceful flight to its fishing places. Many species at risk find sanctuary here, including Blanding's turtle, spotted turtle, black terns and least bitterns, Indiana bats, and ospreys, all protected under the treaties that protect the people. For the Mohawk people, any loss here takes with it a part of culture and the way of living on the land.

Along its way the river curves a border between the US and Canada, surges around islands, and runs through Akwesasne with its 28,000 acres split into the "Canadian side" and the "American side." The line was drawn after the Revolution in the 1783 Treaty of Paris that Great Britain and the newly formed colonies signed to end the war. The people of Akwesasne were told that the border would not affect them and it would be symbolically "lifted twenty feet above the tallest person's head" when they passed through.

The Canadian border curves down below Cornwall Island and instead of running straight through the middle of the river, the line jumps south to encompass part of the reserve's peninsula and St. Regis Village, cutting through the middle of the building where Akwesasne's CKON radio station was built, even and splitting a resident's yard between New York and Ontario. Then the line picks up through Tsi-Snaine, also called Snye, on the southern shore that encompasses it in Quebec.

The border crosses the parking lot of Kanonhkwatshe:ko, Place of Good Medicine, where Canada claims jurisdiction, so it's operated by the Mohawk Council of Akwesasne (MCA), which Canada recognizes. Public health in Canada is through Health Canada, broken down through the two provinces of Ontario and Quebec. On the south shores of the border, public health is through the New York State Department of Health and the US Department of Health and Human Services distributed by the St. Regis Mohawk Tribe (SRMT), which America recognizes.

Driving through the community of Akwesasne, past the shops and signs along State Route 37, one goes by side roads where there are people who can tell you about the changing bird populations, the rooting of invasive plants along the riverbanks, the struggle of black ash trees against emerald ash borers. Wolves were chased away from the forests here. The ravens went with them. Eastern coyotes filtered in, talking to each other in the night hills of the Adirondack Mountains. The ravens returned with them. Bears stay far from the scent of humans, preferring the higher ground of the mountains, but from time to time one will wander through the community.

The signs along Route 37 express the community's divided factions. A "Gambling Is Not Our Tradition" sign is posted up the road from another sign reading "Where the Winning Never Stops," advertising the St. Regis Tribe's Casino Palace that opened in 1999 and the Bingo Palace that opened in 1985. These casinos prosper, earning the state and the tribe revenues of $15 million a year. Another sign reads, "Yes Terrorists Come Thru Akwesasne They are NYS, Border Patrol, ATF, FBI, IRS Etc Etc!!!" One more sign implores "No Drugs."

Being intersected by two federal governments, two provinces, and a state—all claiming jurisdictions, each with their own sets of policies—has presented unique problems. There are separate water and wastewater treatment systems that service Akwesasne but are not connected despite being within feet of each other. There is a broadband initiative being implemented in the southern portion, but one is also needed for the northern portion to support economic development, education, and address other unmet community needs. The community's recreation centers, long-term care facility, and assisted living facility for elders are across the river on the island. Quebec nurses are licensed in Ontario but often must be licensed in both Quebec and Ontario.

Electricity flows into the community from both bordering countries. Quebec portions of Akwesasne receive some of the lowest electric rates in

Canada but the portions in Ontario and New York pay more expensive rates even when two houses are next to each other. There are two police departments patrolling each side, one fire department with three fire stations, and two museum centers.

During a 1990s uprising in the community, outside ambulances refused to enter Akwesasne. A handful of people began the process of getting their own, pushing for their own health care. One ambulance service now operates throughout Akwesasne—in its Quebec, Ontario, and New York state regions. The emergency medical technicians must be aware of where they are at all times because the different jurisdictions prevent certain treatments from being administered in certain areas. These divisions are the result of outside forces.

On the sun-filled morning of September 17, 2010, a ceremony returned a covenant belt of friendship from a museum to the Mohawk community, after more than two centuries absence. The wampum is called the Akwesasne Wolf Belt, representing a covenant made by the Native nations along the St. Lawrence River to protect their communities and work together in friendship. The belt has two human figures clasping hands in the center, embedded in purple wampum on fourteen rows of white beads. Seven purple lines signify what was the Seven Nations, a political union encouraged by French missionaries to the Haudenosaunee. The white row of beads between the purple lines represents a peace path guarded at the east and west by the Wolf Clan, represented by two animal figures.

The sacred wampum was carried from MCA's Ronathanhonni Cultural Center on Cornwall Island and paddled across the south channel of the St. Lawrence Seaway in the lead canoe of Arnold Printup, Historic Preservation Officer for the St. Regis Mohawk Tribe.

The Akwesasne Women's Singers sang. Traditional foods were served. It was a time of nationhood, a reminder that there continues to be a deep, ancient identity despite the border through the community. There is a timeless bond of a shared history.

The people gathered for a celebration, with speakers at the museum, where the treaty belt is displayed, reminding visitors they will always be one nation. Within all the resultant factions of Akwesasne there are those knowing that to abandon their identity is to condemn the next generations.

Half a century ago ships interfered with the courses of the canoes when the St. Lawrence-FDR Power Project pierced the river banks on the St. Lawrence River to create a series of locks and canals, opening markets for international ships to sail from the ocean inland to the Great Lakes. Thomas E. Dewey selected Robert Moses as Power Authority chairman. Moses and his Ontario counterpart, Robert H. Saunders, shook hands and ground was broken on August 10, 1954.

Glossy crows announced the arrival of strangers to the woods. Their twinkling dark eyes watched as worker's hands assaulted their places, pierced the banks with fangs of shovels and moved the ancient compressed rocks in enormous excavations. Blue jays joined the vocal announcements, in the same family as crows, bewildered by trenches eight to twelve stories deep and four miles long. Concrete was poured in and hardened. Shoreline was shredded and laid bare. Wildflowers and the strengths within their leaves lay in the dust. Spawning beds that sustained fish and their young were demolished. More than two hundred farms disappeared. More than 6,500 people had to move.

The hundred-mile drop in the river between eastern Lake Ontario and Massena, New York, just west of Akwesasne, inspired engineers to commandeer rises and falls of water for hydroelectric power. The Long Sault Dam was built about four miles upstream, on Canada's side, to harness the runoff of the waters. Twenty-nine miles upstream the Iroquois Dam and sixteen miles of dikes silenced the fresh, bubbling, oxygen-infused waters of the Long Sault rapids, the twenty-five-mile heartbeat of the river.

Troubled thoughts mounted in the community. Some people drowned because familiar currents now moved differently. Four islands were partially flooded—Adams Island, Toussaint Island, Presquile Island, and Sheek Island. Sands where turtles returned year after year were covered over by heavy sediment. Sheltering places and seeds washed away. Four years of construction caused the waters to spread over one hundred square miles and reshape into Lake St. Lawrence, covering eight villages and burial grounds of relatives.

The Kaniatarowaneneh for centuries brought the Haudenosaunee to lift their minds in thanks for the sturgeon, walleye, pike, and perch, the drinking water, washing water, and blocks of ice cut in winter and covered with sawdust to keep in storage. At all gatherings of the people, they were instructed to turn their minds to the waters to give thanks. No family was ever without food. Even during the Depression era of the US, the pristine waters, clear enough to see to twenty feet below, gave the Mohawk so much bounty that they donated barrels of fish to soup kitchens in the city of New York. But now the dam rose over the landscape at 169 feet tall, 3,200 feet long, and 184 feet wide. Its stark gray dominance on the river was celebrated with a sixty-foot silvery aluminum arch International Friendship Monument placed in the center, flanked by the flags of the two nations. The monument states, "This stone bears witness to the common purpose of two nations whose frontiers are the frontiers of friendship, whose ways are the ways of freedom, and whose works are the works of peace."

The seaway opened on June 26, 1959, creating a coast accessible by oceangoing vessels as long as 730 feet to lake ports such as Buffalo, Cleveland, Toledo, Detroit, Chicago, Milwaukee, Duluth, and Toronto. As the flow left the river, grass flats expanded in the slow-moving water of Lake St. Francis. Migrating fish like sturgeon swam the free flow as they always had, but now hit a block of dam, and struggled to fulfill the instinct within them until it dimmed, leaving them there to die. Perch lost their food and starved, and other fish who eat the perch began dying. Striped bass were bewildered when they saw they'd lost the places of freshwater that earth had given them to spawn and incubate in. The last year a commercial catch of St. Lawrence striped bass was recorded was 1965.

The marshes that had provided fishermen with fish were lost. Where once the people could visit and fill burlap bags with hickory and hazelnuts, there now was a vast pool. No longer could they show their children and grandchildren the bounty that Creator had given. As eels disappeared from the river, an ability to communicate certain ways of fishing and ways of giving thanks diminished in the community. Sights of the eels chopped into pieces drifting all over the water replaced what earlier boat travelers commonly saw: as many as 200 wriggling through the currents.

For healing of any life to take place, there needs to be a secure homeland. Treaty signatories never agreed to separate from rivers, lakes, and earth. Words like "all rights, title to," were not understood by a people who had no concept of buying or selling earth. They didn't agree to forsake giving thanks.

More than five centuries after the Doctrine of Discovery was issued, in 2007 and 2008 the Episcopal Church's Dioceses of Maine and Central New York passed resolutions denouncing the doctrine. They state in part, "That the 76th General Convention repudiates and renounces the Doctrine of Discovery as fundamentally opposed to the Gospel of Jesus Christ and our understanding of the inherent rights that individuals and peoples have received from God, and that this declaration be proclaimed among our churches and shared with the United Nations and all the nations and peoples located within the Episcopal Church's boundaries." The resolution calls on Queen Elizabeth II to repudiate the doctrine and urges that "each diocese within the Episcopal Church be encouraged to reflect upon its own history, in light of these actions[,] and encourage all Episcopalians to seek a greater understanding of the Indigenous Peoples."

Today's Americans and Canadians are not the ones who committed the wrongs of past centuries, but we are the ones who live with the consequences. Just as the sickness in the water was left to us to repair. Collectively, North America's indigenous people hold more natural lands than all the national parks and The Nature Conservancy areas combined. Knowledge of their homelands is increasingly being sought. Students coming out of areas in social or environmental justice issues are likely to work among the original people in equality while churches continue to struggle with relationships. What the stories of the river tell us is how healing builds from a point of common concern when voices are heard.

President Ronald Reagan signed the American Indian Policy in 1983 directing federal agencies to deal with Indian governments on a nation-to-nation basis. The EPA was the first agency to adopt such a policy. The 1972 Clean Water Act that ignored Indian communities was amended in 1987, authorizing the EPA to treat Indian nations as states.

In 1992 the Confederacy sent representatives to the UN Earth Summit in Brazil. The representatives brought the words of the Law's Thanksgiving Address to remind people of their responsibility to the natural world. They shared concerns about the contamination of ancestral lands and the internal tensions it was causing.

After the summit, the Haudenosaunee held a Grand Council to discuss the environmental destruction, the loss of a sustainable economy displaced by gambling and smuggling, and the urgency of problems faced by indigenous peoples everywhere. The Law of Peace taught that the greatest power, that of enacting peace and getting people to put down their weapons, is brought about through unity of people and with justice.

The councils of each of the six nations met, then came together as a Grand Council and agreed to establishing the Haudenosaunee Environmental Task Force (HETF), composed of leaders and scientists chosen from each of the nations. Henry Lickers, Akwesasne's first director of an environmental department, became the science cochair, and Oren Lyons, Seneca and faithkeeper in the Onondaga Nation, became the political cochair.

"If sustainable development is to succeed, it must become the concern and commitment not just of governments, but of all segments of society," they stated. Working with the UN, England's Cambridge University, the US Environmental Protection Agency, and Indigenous Development International, the Confederacy penned the Haudenosaunee Environmental Restoration Strategy—"An Indigenous Strategy for Sustainability."

HETF reminded that the ship of the EPA's water quality standards was not to steer the canoe of collective knowledge of lands and culture. Original treaties of friendship now paved the way for two different governments to work together. When applied to the environment, the EPA brings people from the canoe into the ship to show how they create environmental standards. The people from the canoe can modify this to their own standards suitable for their own lifeways.

The law they'd been given now gave a way to respond to today's world. Peacemaker said, "Now you are all standing upon the land and you shall be tall tree trunks, rooted tree trunks; and as to that, everyone shall be on the same level among all of you tall tree trunks, and this is what it means, for you to be tall trees; you are the ones who will stand in front—at your backs they stand, your people—but as to you, you chiefs, it is on the same level that you stand which means that your various nations are all equal with respect to your power."

Jesus had led people of both cultures to the water to begin an equal relationship. From the longhouse, the spiritual center of the people's community, come the people who go to the rivers and the lakes, seeking partnerships with others who share concerns for universal well-being, arising from the giving of thanks.

The St. Lawrence River, with jurisdictions on both sides of the border, is the only Area of Concern in the United States that includes a Native territory. The goal to restore the river's health would have to be shared. An increasing number of universities were proposing research at Akwesasne, but in the past researchers were culturally insensitive or didn't share findings or funding with the reserve. In response, the reserve developed Protocols for Review of Scientific and Environmental Research so that research at Akwesasne was done only with the input and consent of the community. The protocol was based on a circle of respect, equity, and empowerment that would benefit the community with the information gleaned in research.

The low-cost hydroelectric power had attracted a number of industries. These included Reynolds Metal Company, an aluminum smelter established on 1,600 acres bounded by the river on the north and the Raquette River on the south; General Motors Powertrain, an automobile parts manufacturer on 270 acres east of Massena; Alcoa on 3,500 acres bounded by the river on the north; and the Massena Power Canal, situated on the southwest side of the river with the Grasse River on the southeast. To the north, across the river, Domtar Paper was emitting an average of 380 pounds of noxious yellow-gray sulfur fumes into the air each day.

From the ship's perspective, a fish advisory was a good thing. It prevented people from eating contaminated foods. But from the canoe's perspective, the advisory had a profound effect on the ability of the canoe to maintain its course.

Just two years after the fish advisory was issued, after fishermen left their nets in their yards, gambling and smuggling replaced the lost revenues. Families divided against each other as some supported gaming and others resisted its nontraditional ploys. By 1989, there were a half dozen high stakes bingo parlors and casinos along Route 37. Hundreds of Mohawk supporters and opponents exploded at each other. By March 1990 the opponents erected barricades to prevent gamblers from coming onto the reservation. Cars were torched, houses shot at, farms burned. An international web of smuggling networked Akwesasne's highways and rivers, bringing AK-47 and M16 automatic rifles for shootouts. By May, a raid of 250 state police, FBI agents, and IRS agents was resisted and resulted in a blockade outside of the reservation, cutting off all media, delivery, and services for several months. Mohawk women and men who relied on local fish for much of their diet had their consumption of them reduced to about two meals a month. By 1990, half the people over age forty became diabetic, a disease unheard of in the community fifty years ago. Hypothyroidism and upper respiratory illness came upon the people. The loss of culture has left more than twenty percent of American Indians victimized by this growing epidemic. Among Aboriginal people in Canada rates of disease are three to five times higher than that of the general population.

The people had been told these things would come upon them. They were warned because they would need to make decisions about the future of their people.

In 1802 the state of New York passed legislation recognizing three trustees and a clerk whom the Mohawk chose to give a voice to the people on the American side of their territory. The traditional role of roiane continued. These people are known as life chiefs. Some 1,100 years ago,

Peacemaker and Hiawatha organized the Mohawk families into three clans—Turtle, Wolf and Bear—each with a roiane so there would be extended families and balanced governance. The Great Law unified the Mohawk Council with roiane from each clan, who meet as a government in a longhouse. These are lifelong positions. When a leader passes, the title remains in the circle of roiane to continue serving through the generations, just as Hiawatha's did.

The Peacemaker's traditional longhouse of the Confederacy is nestled in a field down a side road on the New York side of the reserve. The longhouse is fresh with the scent of pine used to build it, its roof and floor representing the sky and earth. Women enter the western door. Men enter the eastern door.

But the US recognizes only the three trustees, and gave the leaders the name "chief." The council evolved into the St. Regis Tribal Council, with three elected chiefs and three elected subchiefs, each with a term of three years. They are federally recognized on the American side of the Mohawk territory and hold rights according to the Clean Water, Clean Air, and various other Acts.

Across the river in 1884, on the Canadian side of the reserve, the Canadian Indian Advancement Act enforced the Mohawk Council of Akwesasne. Many petitions of the roiane went to Canada requesting polishing of the rights of treaties that state that the border will not interfere with their reserve. The petitions stated that the Indians throw off all other laws and put their own over every other for the benefit of their people and recalled that they had their own leadership of the people. Canada responded and prevailed with weapons, death, and jail sentences.

A statue of Jake Fire stands on Cornwall Island in remembrance of the ancestor who was shot and killed on May 1, 1899 when he tried to protect his brother from Indian agents who came to enforce the elected system. The people consistently voiced their desire to keep their own governance. Headlines in the March 30 *Massena Observer* read "Indians on the War Path." Agents had come and smashed down the door and an election was held under gunpoint, yet the headlines in the May 8 *Massena Observer* read "More Trouble at the St. Regis Reservation" over a story about their "resistance to the law."

The date is recognized every year and was chosen as the day to begin the Unity Rally in 2009 when the Canadian government refused to speak with them about arming border guards on their territory.

In 1834 the Mohawk Council of Chiefs was asked if there was any problem with building control structures on the rivers. The elders told them this would impact the blue stem meadows, spawning grounds, and marshes. A growing population was excavating hundreds of indigenous sites every year, old places of meaning, of spiritual renewals, and of burials. By 1852 the Mohawk found it necessary to conduct an environmental assessment. They again warned the newcomers of the consequences of their plans for the land. They held council on October 24, 1894 and agreed they needed to reestablish their own form of government. They sent the resolution to Ottawa in April:

> Brother, Whereas We the undersigned have taken into serious consideration to cause it to declare our grievance, and to lay before Your Excellency that our anxiety is to be exempted of the Elective System form of Councilors, of which it is injurious to our nationality to which it is not calculated to promote our welfare, of which we have not derived of any benefit since the elective form of council existed among the Indians of Canada, and therefore that we thought that it is high time to cause it to lay before Your Excellency's serious consideration, that we know every nation is made distinct through by the Great Spirit's will. It appears to us that it is extremely hard to be governed by a distinct nationality of course it has been prophesied before the advent of white men that mighty power is coming from the East to govern the country of the aborigines, and plunder their national freedom. Brother, the prophecy is handed down from father to son and up to the present age and therefore to compare the prophecy and actions of the Canadian Government that the Indians are looked upon as minors, and treat them as such, for it is plainly to be seen that the Superintendent General of Indian Affairs has the full power to control and management of the lands and property of the Indians of Canada.

Today's council is comprised of twelve chiefs, four chiefs from each of three electoral districts of Snye, Kawehno:ke (Cornwall Island) and Kana:takon (St. Regis Village). A majority vote elects a Grand Chief to the council for a three-year term. The federal government's Indian and Northern Affairs Canada agency provides services such as education, health care, environmental care, and welfare to this government and community members of this government.

Today, Akwesasne's 13,000 community members live with this.

There were attempts to dismantle the St. Regis Tribal Council in 1949 and 1979. In the 1990s legislation was introduced to rescind the law that ignored their traditional government but New York's Governor Pataki would not endorse it.

The book of authority used by the churches reminds each generation, "If my people, which are called by my name, shall humble themselves, and pray, and seek my face, and turn from their wicked ways, then will I hear from heaven, and will forgive their sin, and will heal their land" (2 Chr 7:14).

The writer of Psalm 143:8 implored, "Let the morning bring me word of your unfailing love, for I have put my trust in you. Show me the way I should go, for to you I entrust my life."

God replies: "Return to me and I will return to you" (Mal 3:7).

When Job was so afflicted by loss of everything in his life, his thoughts remained centered: "He spreads out the northern skies over empty space; he suspends the earth over nothing. He wraps up the waters in his clouds, yet the clouds do not burst under their weight. He covers the face of the full moon, spreading his clouds over it. The pillars of the heavens quake, aghast at his rebuke. By his power he churned up the sea. . . . By his breath the skies become fair. . . . And these are but the outer fringe of his works; how faint the whisper we hear of him! How then can we understand the thunder of his power?" (Job 26:7–9,11–14).

God disregarded all the attempts of the counselors in Job 38 and 39 and pointed attention to his reign over creation.

> By what way is the light parted, which scatter the east wind upon the earth? Who has divided a watercourse for the overflowing of waters, or a way for the lightning of thunder; to cause it to rain on the earth, where no man is; on the wilderness, wherein there is no man; to satisfy the desolate and waste ground; and to cause the bud of the tender herb to spring forth? Has the rain a father? Or who has begotten the drops of dew? Out of whose womb came the ice? And the hoary frost of heaven, who has gendered it? The waters are hid as with a stone, and the face of the deep is frozen. Can you bind the sweet influences of Pleiades, or loose the bands of Orion? Can you bring forth Mazzaroth in his season? Or can you guide Arcturus with his sons? Know you the ordinances of heaven? Can you set the dominion thereof in the earth? Can you lift up your voice to the clouds, that abundance of waters may cover you? Can you send lightnings, that they may go, and say unto you, Here we are? Who has put wisdom in the inward parts? Or who

> has given understanding to the heart? Who can number the clouds in wisdom? Or who can stay the bottles of heaven, When the dust grows into hardness, and the clods cleave fast together? Will you hunt the prey for the lion? Or fill the appetite of the young lions, when they crouch in their dens, and abide in the covert to lie in wait? Who provides for the raven his food? When his young ones cry unto God, they wander for lack of meat. Have you given the horse strength? Have you clothed his neck with thunder? Can you make him afraid as a grasshopper? The glory of his nostrils *is* terrible. He paws in the valley, and rejoices in his strength: he goes on to meet the armed men. He mocks at fear, and is not affrighted; neither turns he back from the sword. The quiver rattles against him, the glittering spear and the shield. He swallows the ground with fierceness and rage: neither believes he that it is the sound of the trumpet. He says among the trumpets, Ha, ha; and he smells the battle afar off, the thunder of the captains, and the shouting. Does the hawk fly by your wisdom, and stretch her wings toward the south? Does the eagle mount up at your command, and make her nest on high? She dwells and abides on the rock, upon the crag of the rock, and the strong place. From there she seeks the prey, and her eyes behold afar off.

God pointed to the creation as evidence of a greater plan that we are too young to understand.

That he gave us the sun's warmth, the cycle of replenishing rainwater, all the foods we need for health, brought thanks from languages worldwide, and gave rise to joy in an extended covenant to bring eternal salvation. Voices rise in shared worship recognizing a shared need. Redemption means there is a way back to again know relationship with our Creator.

After Job prayed for his counselors, reestablishing good relationship, he was again blessed. We are to put aside weapons of blame and accusations as Peacemaker had symbolized by burying weapons of war beneath a tree where water could wash them away.

When the Great Law was used as a blueprint for the US Constitution, the word "responsibility" was changed to "rights." We may have the right to take all of the fish in the river—but we have responsibility to help the fish continue so they're here for the next generation.

Every year the Akwesasne fishermen had brought in the fish. Families got together. They'd have a wonderful picnic because someone brought in the fish. But now everywhere the fish are contaminated.

A fish advisory was issued. Fishermen cut their nets, abandoned their gear in their yards. The sense of community was lost. There goes some of your culture. There go some of those beautiful thoughts.

Gone were the centuries when relationships between elders and youth, neighbors and those across the river happened naturally day-to-day, while planting seeds, harvesting in fall, sewing clothes, building homes, walking to the cook house, and simply isiting with each other. Language is an integral part of culture than can be restored. Akwesasne began restoration with their own language for their children and children's children to hold.

There were no textbooks to pull off the shelf. They had to create a whole new way that would bring elders together with youth and structure it for others to learn their mother tongue. Language immersion programs, signage in communities, music, CDs, songs, art, and videos made by the students were all incorporated to bring language to life. This generation did their part, put into place a foundation so that each succeeding generation will expand it and speak more and more of their natural language. In the way of nature, they became the balance to that loss, the way dock leaves grow next to stinging nettles and soothe with a mild astringent.

Human rights in recent times has linked up with the rise of language revitalization. Maori, spoken by indigenous people of New Zealand, was revived by a successful immersion program that has been copied around the world as language instructors meet to exchange ideas about teaching. Hawaii, Wales, Galicia, and Catalonia have followed. Hebrew was revived as the national language of Israel even after there were no longer fluent native speakers.

In Ireland the government supports efforts to revitalize its first language, overcoming the past's bans and stigmatism and the immigration of thousands to America. Heritage from the land of origin has driven human groups through all history. Until 2000 Deutschland (meaning the Land of the Germans) gave citizenship only to those with German bloodlines.

At the 2010 UN gathering of the Permanent Forum of Indigenous Issues, voices from around the world's 370 million indigenous people shared their experiences. The forum is comprised of representatives from North America, Eastern Europe, the Pacific, the Arctic, Central and South America, the Caribbean, Asia, and Africa, places where the Doctrine of Discovery was used as a destroyer.

Azure Peacock, representing the Australian Youth Caucus, urged the UN to encourage states to include the views of indigenous people as climate change and environmental degradation become more of a concern.

From Bolivia, Sergio Hinojosa said the first peoples were recovering their identities and the corresponding rights to relationship with Mother Earth were being recognized. Kaab Malik from the Indigenous Peoples Survival Foundation was concerned about the devastating impact of environmental change forcing people to change their traditional ways of life in his country, Pakistan. The Vice-Minister of Venezuela, Carlos Samara, proposed education about concepts of the Western world and revitalization efforts in communities such as those in Africa where they rebuild from the destruction of the capitalist world.

Hinduoumarou Hindou reported that twenty-eight indigenous leaders from fifteen African countries had gathered in Mali to create a plan to implement the Declaration on Human Rights. From China, Zhou Ningyu said government was meeting the challenge of educating youth in remote mountain places with boarding schools.

A network has formed around the world, facing common challenges together, finding support in each other, encouragement and strength. As destruction pulses its way into the world these networks prepare the way for a body of people labeled Christians, a name meaning the redeemed who even in suffering are covered with God's Spirit.

A foresight of the last days that will come on people everywhere is told in the recording of the deposed high priest Jason, returning from Egypt. He gathered a force of soldiers and attacked Jerusalem. He executed many Jews. Second Maccabees 5:11-14 describes it: "There was a massacre of young and old, a killing of women and children, a slaughter of virgins and infants. In the space of three days, eighty thousand were lost, forty thousand meeting a violent death, and the same number being sold into slavery." The text continues:

> Not long after this the king sent an Athenian senator to force the Jews to abandon the customs of their ancestors and live no longer by the laws of God; also to profane the temple in Jerusalem and dedicate it to Olympian Zeus, and that on Mount Gerizim to Zeus the Hospitable, as the inhabitants of the place requested. . . . They also brought into the temple things that were forbidden, so that the altar was covered with abominable offerings prohibited by the laws. A man could not keep the sabbath or celebrate the traditional feasts, nor even admit that he was a Jew. At the suggestion of the

citizens of Ptolemais, a decree was issued ordering the neighboring Greek cities to act in the same way against the Jews: oblige them to partake of the sacrifices, and put to death those who would not consent to adopt the customs of the Greeks. It was obvious, therefore, that disaster impended. Thus, two women who were arrested for having circumcised their children were publicly paraded about the city with their babies hanging at their breasts and then thrown down from the top of the city wall. Others, who had assembled in nearby caves to observe the sabbath in secret, were betrayed to Philip and all burned to death.

Trauma is prophesied to come on all believers of Christ, a challenge that will unify us under one concern for the living water of Christ. The living water is like the river, bringing people across all heritages and backgrounds, each with their knowledge, to focus on a flow that will bring health to all who depend on it. Water is life. The Mohawk bring their traditional knowledge and base decisions on how it will affect each element of the Thanksgiving Address. Western education brings its science and together they form a collective resource for all the elements. Water baptism symbolizes our crossing the sea that separates us from heaven. This ceiling was not passable until the Lord Christ completed his mission on earth. "And he said unto them, You are from beneath; I am from above: you are of this world; I am not of this world" (John 8:23).

Paul used an analogy to describe our limited perception here on earth: "For now we see only a reflection as in a mirror; then we shall see face to face. Now I know in part; then I shall know fully, even as I am fully known" (1 Cor 13:12). We are known fully by God as we struggle to find our way, but we are as yet unable to fully know the Great Mystery spoken of by the Native nations. Genesis 1:6–8 refers to the creation of the dark glass above us. "And God said, Let there be a firmament in the midst of the waters, and let it divide the waters from the waters. And God made the firmament, and divided the waters which were under the firmament from the waters which were above the firmament: and it was so. And God called the firmament Heaven. And the evening and the morning were the second day."

The firmament between the two waters is a place for the sun, moon, and stars. "And God said, Let there be lights in the firmament of the heaven to divide the day from the night; and let them be for signs, and for seasons, and for days, and years" (Gen 1:14). "Praise him, you heavens of heavens, and you waters that be above the heavens" (Ps 148:4). These two levels are our sky. "And God said, let the waters bring forth abundantly the moving creature that has life, and fowl that may fly above the earth in the open firmament of heaven" (Gen 1:20). Above where the birds fly, Genesis 1:14 tells us there are lights to divide day from night, signs for seasons, days, and years. "And God called the firmament heaven." Above this is the sea below the throne of God that resembles ice, frozen water. "And before the throne there was a sea of glass like unto crystal: and in the midst of the throne, and round about the throne, were four beasts full of eyes before and behind" (Rev 4:6). The separation will no longer exist after the Lord returns to earth. John said, "And I saw a new heaven and a new earth: for the first heaven and the first earth were passed away; and there was no more sea" (Rev 21:1).

When the Haudenosaunee built the longhouse of white pine it was full of symbolism. The floor represents earth, the high ceiling represents the sky world, the walls the four directions. Other peoples's architecture holds similar meanings. The Lakota, for instance, construct tipis with the poles aligning to the star constellations above. The design of Solomon's temple, described in 1 Kings 7:23 and 2 Chronicles 4:2, with the Molten Sea between the altar and the most holy place, represents the barrier where sacrifice is made, and, in a Christian reading, the barrier between the world below where Christ would be born and crucified and the world above, at the throne of God in the third heaven. The veil tearing when Jesus died represented a way made to cross that barrier that also led the peoples of the world to each other. The Apostle Paul saw this when he wrote in 2 Corinthians 12:2, "I knew a man in Christ about fourteen years ago, whether in the body, I cannot tell; or whether out of the body, I cannot tell: God knows; such a one caught up to the third heaven." "And they saw the God of Israel: and there was under his feet as it were a paved work of a sapphire stone, and as it were the body of heaven in his clearness" (Exod 24:10). John's vision in Revelation 15:2 describes the boundary as crystal or smooth glass. "And I saw as it were a sea of glass mingled with fire: and them that had gotten the victory over the beast, and over his image, and over his mark, and over the number of his name, stand on the sea of glass, having the harps of God." It's a place of song.

4

Two-Row Wampum

Ask the Lord for rain in the springtime; it is the Lord who makes the storm clouds. He gives showers of rain to men, and plants of the field to everyone.

ZECHARIAH 10:1

PEACEMAKER POINTED TO FOUR white roots of the white pine tree extending to earth's four corners and said, "Anyone who desires peace can follow the roots to their source and find shelter under the Great Tree." Centuries after the veil was torn in the temple when Christ was crucified, the people, animals, and plants around the world all began to meet on the North American continent. In the Netherlands the Dutch lived at the mouths of rivers offering routes between the North Sea and Atlantic Ocean and launched an economy of trade. The English too found trade in Indian country. As these ancestors rose from the Hudson River in North America, they met the Native peoples known as the Haudenosaunee on the shores.

When traders arrived and relationship began, the newcomers experienced the Edge of the Woods Ceremony. Over time the Confederacy saw that their different thinking wouldn't graft into the Hiawatha Belt that linked their nations under the Great Law. Needing a way to live side by side, they extended the concepts of the Great Peace into a new treaty known as the Two-Row, commissioning each to have an understanding of the other's needs.

The Two-Row Wampum, called the Kaswentha, is a treaty belt between two societies that recognizes their distinct elements of lifestyle and governance. Its white quahog beads are the river of life. Two purple rows, separated by three rows of white beads, run parallel through its length. The purple rows signify two vessels traveling down the river together. One vessel is for the European ship that later became the Canadians and Americans. The other vessel is a canoe for the Haudenosaunee and other Native peoples.

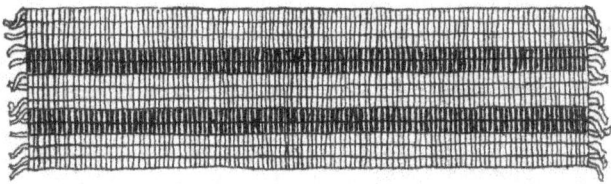

The three white rows that separate the vessels symbolize skennen (peace), kariwiio (a good mind), and kasastensera (strength). These three concepts keep the ship and canoe close, yet at a respectful distance from each other. The purpose of this treaty is that as we travel the river of life together independently, the ship and canoe are to help each other from time to time. We are not to try to steer the other's vessel. Treaties signed five centuries ago were signed with thoughts of future generations, knowing what they each did would affect the other. "And as to your own fireside, never consider only yourself, you must always remember them, the old people, the younger people and the children, and those still in the earth, yet unborn, and always you will take into account everyone's well-being, that of the ongoing families, so that they may continue to survive, your grandchildren."

Spreading a new faith established in the covenant with God, the Apostle Paul visited the Corinthian people and set forth the need to have cultural respect between peoples, telling them, "When I am with the Gentiles who do not follow the Jewish law, I too live apart from that law so I can bring them to Christ. But I do not ignore the law of God; I obey the law of Christ. When I am with those who are weak, I share their weakness, for I want to bring the weak to Christ. Yes, I try to find common ground with everyone, doing everything I can to save some" (1 Cor 9:21–22).

In Galatians 6 we find Paul saying that cultural rituals shouldn't be a point of distraction. Circumcision and uncircumcision are not the point. God has already accomplished reconciling the world to himself. The message to be carried is about this hope. Each is to continue on as they were, whether Jew or Gentile. He does not seek to destroy culture created in diversity, a harmony of races, rich and poor, young and old, all called to the transformation. It's part of the contentment Paul speaks of, while never giving up his own deep roots in heritage.

In Romans 3:1–2 he says, "What advantage then has the Jew, or what is the profit of circumcision? Much in every way! Chiefly because to them were committed the oracles of God." His Hebrew people shared a similar relationship to land as the North American people. "The earth is the LORD's, and everything in it, the world, and all who live in it" (Ps 24:1). Paul takes down the wall between cultures in 1 Corinthians 7 and 8. In crushing poverty, facing arrest and death by a hostile religious response, the people gave to the needs of those they hadn't met, bonded by being called to serve the same God, becoming living stones, building a new people determinedly passing on the knowledge of Christ so we would have it today. After the veil tore and people moved toward forming a global church, missionaries in the beginning failed to recognize the difference between culture and Christianity. Believing in divine leading they came carrying Bibles. "Praise the LORD from the earth, you great sea creatures and all ocean depths, lightning and hail, snow and clouds, stormy winds that do his bidding, you mountains and all hills, fruit trees and all cedars, wild animals and all cattle, small creatures and flying birds" (Ps 148:7–10). Even the trees of the field clap their hands (Isa 55:12). But differing views on relationship to land inhibited mutual understanding as struggles to survive on a new continent took precedence. Where the earliest missionaries brought the cross, capitalism and paternalistic structures of groups, from governments and agencies to churches, followed.

Like a stone tossed into water, this scattered the people like droplets. By the 1600s, Jesuits, being called the Black Robes, arrived from the mistral winds and set up stations with the Mi'qmac in Nova Scotia and steadily traveled inland to the other peoples. The Huron's 30,000-person population was slashed to ten thousand by plagues brought by the French in the 1630s. The Huron met with Haudenosaunee leadership to move toward a conciliation of peace, but the Jesuits prevented this. Again in 1640 the Haudenosaunee met with the Huron to establish peace, and again the Jesuits thwarted their efforts. Following the water down the Mohawk River, Jesuits travelled to the Mohawk Valley in 1642 to begin converting the people into the Catholic system. After the army burned the Mohawk's bark-covered homes and destroyed their winter supply of food in 1666 the Mohawk made a peace under duress that resulted in the missionaries gaining more access to their territory. Many Jesuits were martyred for their efforts but not for speaking the name of Jesus. It was in wars, loss of homeland, sudden competition for the fur trade with neighboring tribes, all fueled by the coming of missionaries bringing disease, that developed into mockery of Indian lifeways and disruption of their families.

The mission established in 1755 in Akwesasne has integrated into the Mohawk landscape a memorial of the deaths during war, the divisions the European fighting caused in the community, the 1829 smallpox epidemic, typhus and cholera epidemics in 1832, and other disasters. A side road following along the St. Regis River as it finds its way from the Adirondack Mountains into the St. Lawrence leads to the quiet shore called Kana:takon, the village, sometimes called St. Regis Village in Quebec. One of the oldest buildings in the region, the stone mission church, stands on the peninsula, its steeple built toward the northeast and reaching above the trees. Seven generations ago, men, women, and children among the Mohawk helped construct the building from stone, learning masonry, quarrying tons of limestone, and floating logs down from the Thousand Islands, completing the building in 1795. Sermons were conducted in the Mohawk language and today occasionally masses, wakes, and funerals are still conducted in Mohawk. Gregorian chants and hymns translated into Mohawk by French priests two centuries ago are sometimes sung by choirs. Inside pillars are carved with the bear, wolf, and turtle that are symbols of the Mohawk clans. At times traditions meld, and people smudge burnt sage to purify themselves before entering mass. Old stories tell that the church was built atop a longhouse and across the river from a burial ground. Tombstones marked in Mohawk were once piled next to the sacristy. In nights past dozens of lights on the bow of dozens of flat-bottom boats were seen out on the river as the people used long twelve-foot spears to harvest the fish. The St. Regis Island can be seen out in the river, unchanged except for the waters now flowing more slowly since the seaway was built.

In the 1990s, when the old church needed repairs, a group of Mohawk raised $150,000 by holding craft fairs, auctions, raffles, and other events. The series of priests who served from the pulpit are part of the landscape's memory, as they were there with the people through ice jams, floods, and earthquakes. Father Moise Mainville, 1883 to 1895, testified about conditions in Akwesasene to a state commission in 1888. Father J.P. Bourget followed and for forty-two years carried a passion for the Mohawk language and education for the youth. People's memories are varied, from being forced to attend church as a child to embracing the religion today. Behind the church, the summer sun still gazes on generations of children as they swing out from a rope hanging from a tree and splash into the river's refreshing waters. Thompson's Marina is adjacent, offering boats and fuel. Upriver is the Mohawk island where Canada set a customs facility, where once the Mohawk had hunted and fished, traveling freely across the river in a land lush with provision. Palisaded villages were once arranged on this peninsula, with a clear view of any arrivals along the water. It was a place ideal for conducting trade. The church became a landmark. There was a large wharf on the peninsula where steamships from Montreal would dock and pick up cargo and passengers. A blockhouse and a set of piers was used by the authorities to hold the flotillas of logs that came from the Adirondack lumber camps. About five feet below the river's surface rectangular sections of concrete, once part of the docks, can still be seen. It's easy to imagine the lone canoe out on the river in times past.

Whip-poor-wills bringing their mellow song to the spring nights are few now, 97 percent declined since 1983. Gray-brown feathers marked with black blend into nests among the leaves of forest floors where they lay their eggs in phase with the moon's cycles so the hatchlings are born before a full moon, providing light for hunting insects.

The land now holds new bird songs. New flowers and grasses choke out the natural species. Insects fell trees and sculpt a new horizon. Corn has changed with genetic modifications. Domestic animals stamped down the soils, new shoots of plants couldn't grow, and the soil couldn't hold as much water. The land's use changed, with it no longer under the ethics of indigenous gardening that doesn't change a place of earth, but instead collects seeds and nurtures what belongs in an area.

As the St. Lawrence River flows over the earth, evoking memories of the people spearing eels, salmon, catfish, and pike, and of a time when the water drew moose, deer, bear, and beaver, the Thanksgiving Address continues to be upheld. The leafy jewels blossoming across the terrain signal the time when groups of birds arrive from the south, gatherings of cranes, swans, ducks, geese, and loons in abundance.

"The heavens declare the glory of God; the skies proclaim the work of his hands. Day after day they pour forth speech; night after night they display knowledge. There is no speech or language where their voice is not heard. Their voice goes out into all the earth, their words to the ends of the world," the psalm proclaims (19:1–4). This wisdom is in all cultures. There is evidence of the power of our emotions on water, showing that exposing water to the vibrations of harsh feelings, thoughts, words, music, or pictures of people standing by it breaks the beautiful crystals of freezing water into unformed shapes. The same power, using beautiful words, songs, and prayers, showed the result of our state of mind reflected in the water. The quality improved. Perfectly symmetrical crystals formed.

Neuropsychology too is discovering that persons afflicted with illness who believe in a compassionate Christ have better recovery rates than those who believe God is angry. "Whatever things are true, whatever things are honest, whatever things are just, whatever things are pure, whatever things are lovely, whatever things are of good report; if there be any virtue, and if there be any praise, think on these things," Philippians 4:8 instructs.

In 1 Cor 12:18, the apostle of Christ proclaimed, "There are different kinds of gifts but the same Spirit. But in fact God has arranged the parts in the body, every one of them, just as he wanted them to be. If they were all one part, where would the body be? As it is, there are many parts, but one body." The verse reflects creation's intent, each diverse life-form serving to keep the whole continuing for a thousand generations.

The prophets had described this faith as a tree that birds of every kind will seek. They sing different songs rising from a diversity of peoples. He is the desire of all the nations (Hag 2:7).

"Let the heavens rejoice, let the earth be glad; let the sea resound, and all that is in it. Let the fields be jubilant, and everything in them; let all the trees of the forest sing for joy. Let all creation rejoice before the LORD, for he comes, he comes to judge the earth" (Ps 96:13). Psalms 86, 97, and 98 tell us to sing a new song, a song that rises wherever Jesus goes.

As a man Christ had sung the songs the people he was born among had carried for two thousand years. In the years before he faced the cross, he gathered with his disciples in the upper room and sang the Passover psalms: "The Lord is my strength and song; and he is become my salvation" (Ps 118:14) and the song of Moses (Exod 15:2) and of the prophets (Isa 12:2). He sang the songs of his own story, seated on God's right hand (Ps

110:1), ascending to the hill of the Lord (Ps 24:3), where the everlasting gates are thrown open (Ps 24:10).

When he was lifted on the cross, he gazed over the people, filled with compassion and a sense of completion. In heaven the angels waited for his return. We are invited. "Enter into his gates with thanksgiving, and into his courts with praise: be thankful unto him, and bless his name" (Ps 100:4).

The element that unites people groups around the world is the agreement that we are to be thankful. A church holiday can see some two billion believers from every church denomination worshiping in one accord.

On May 17, 2013 Mohawk roiane and 500 young and old Haudenosaunee marched across both spans of the Seaway International Bridge to hand deliver another request for a meeting with Prime Minister Stephen Harper. The sound of their traditional water drums led voices joined in ancient song. It remains an ongoing issue, the division through their territory that prohibits them the right to travel back and forth freely, inherent rights that are more ancient than the newcomer's laws occupying land far from their own lands of origin.

They delivered the letter to the CBSA regional director, outlining concerns and asking that the letter be passed along to the Prime Minister as a first step toward revisiting treaties. They are still on their land. They still speak their language. They practice their customs. MCA opted out of Canada's Indian Act to build a relationship on a genuine government-to-government basis, not on a series of laws inflicted on the people.

Smoke from sage rose as prayer through the sky as Tadodaho Sid Hill explained how they'd been trying to meet with the government for a long time. There's been more alleged mistreatment since the customs offices were moved from their island in 2009 to Ontario's shores.

The generations have carried this request for relationship for more than two centuries. Consider a letter from Mohawk leadership dated April 26, 1895, to "His Excellency Governor General of Canada":

> Brother, Whereas We the undersigned have taken into serious consideration to cause it to declare our grievance, and to lay before Your Excellency that our anxiety is to be exempted of the Elective System form of Councilors, of which it is injurious to our nationality to which it is not calculated to promote our welfare, of which we have not derived of any benefit since the elective form of council existed among the Indians of Canada, and therefore that we thought that it is high time to cause it to lay before Your Excellency's serious consideration, that we know

every nation is made distinct through by the Great Spirit's will. We all know that the old times according to the Bible that the whole earth was one Language and of one speech therefore the Lord came down to see the City and the tower which the children of men builded, and the Lord confounded their language, and scattered them abroad from thence upon the face of all the earth. It appears to us that it is extremely hard to be governed by a distinct nationality of course it has been prophesied before the advent of white men that mighty power is coming from the East to govern the country of the aborigines, and plunder their national freedom. Brother, the prophecy is handed down from father to son and up to the present age. And therefore to compare the prophecy and actions of the Canadian Government that the Indians are looked upon as minors, and treat them as such, for it is plainly to be seen that the Superintendent General of Indian Affairs has the full power to control and management of the lands and property of the Indians of Canada. Brother, we have counciled and put our heads together, to re-establish of our former customs of creating chiefs according to our own clans, and the forthcoming chiefs are already selected and you are to know them in the future to do business between the Government and us the Iroquois of St. Regis. And we therefore give you the resolution passed in our Council October 24, 1894. We therefore give you the names of whom is selected to be fit proper persons to be created Chiefs selected according to our classes. Your Excellency may understand the above stated names of the women's side that they hold the symbolic totems of which they have the right to select their sachems.

"If therefore you are presenting your offering at the altar, and there remember that your brother has something against you, leave your offering there before the altar, and go your way; first be reconciled to your brother, and then come and present your offering" (Matt 5:23–24).

When leadership fought for decades to have a voice in the policies affecting their people, they were taking the responsibility for the broken relationship. "And if your brother sins, go and reprove him in private; if he listens to you, you have won your brother" (Matt 18:15).

One of many pleas throughout the years, this too was ignored. There are about 6,500 spoken languages in today's world. In all of these, our Creator's name epitomizes our relationship to him. In the Bible this relationship is described in many different references: Beginning and End; Bishop of Souls; Branch; Breath of Life; Bridegroom; Bright Morning Star; Author of our faith, Author of Peace; Dayspring; Desired of All Nations; Counselor;

Eternal Spirit; Deliverer; Fountain of Living Waters; Gentle Whisper; Hiding Place; Hope; Living Water; Loving-kindness; Maker; Mediator; Refiner's Fire; Jehovah; Cornerstone; Spirit of Truth; the Way; Wonderful; Wall of Fire; Consuming Fire; Creator; and Ancient of Days.

In Mohawk, this relationship is described as Sonkwaiatison: You Who Gave Me Life. The Indian governance is designed to get warring factions to put down their weapons and reason together, a practice that would promote rights for all indigenous peoples. Peace is not just the absence of war, it is a way of being that promotes our interactions. Power is not a military power, it is the spiritual and political strength that unifies when people are treating each other fairly.

In 2009, Steven Newcomb, Oren Lyons, and Tonya Gonnella Frichner talked about bringing up the Doctrine of Discovery at the UN's Indigenous Forum. Information about the doctrine was requested in the eighth session. One of the sixteen members of the forum, Frichner, from the Onondaga Nation and representing the United States, is an attorney and founder of the American Indian Law Alliance. She reported that a preliminary study of the impact of the Doctrine of Discovery presented support to convene an expert group conducted by a representative of the seven regions of earth identified by the Permanent Forum.

Uganda representative Margaret Lokawua said tradition had been scorned and destroyed and needed to be restored by the people. From Morocco, Hassan Id Balkassm described the European exploitation in Northern Africa. Out of fear of punishment, he spoke his language only at home. Balkassm was jailed for a week for placing a slogan in his language in the window of his law office. Reconciliation committees are meeting in his region. The intergenerational grief caused by the schools in America and Canada had been studied, finding that those who had a parent who attended the schools were far more depressed. They were denied affection as youngsters, because the parents were not naturally affectionate. These offspring also had a greater sensitivity to traumas and discrimination, aware of what their parents had experienced. Aboriginal young of parents of residential schools are at nearly twice the risk of hepatitis C infection as the general population. The parents had left the residential institutions carrying rage and grief that had grown deep without ever being comforted. Carrying what they knew, abuse and violence, led their numbers in prisons to steadily increase. By 1982, colonization practices had produced arrest rates of American Indians eleven times higher than those of non-Natives and three times higher than those of blacks, according to the National Minority Advisory Council on Criminal Justice. America, so proud of its freedoms, would be the country that built the most prisons. There are more than seventy state prisons now standing in New York state.

Hearing the stories of their mothers and fathers, grandmothers and grandfathers, who may have been as young as three years old when they were removed to residential schools, afflicted another generation. Some were told that their parents did not want them. Stories tell of arriving, crying in a strange place, not knowing why they were sent, being told by school staff and clergy to be quiet, you are staying here. The were made to grow crops and tend animals. They got little academic education, saw deaths of other children in massive numbers, made friends with those raped, and were punished for speaking their own language. The Two-Row Wampum had not been respected. Coming out of the years of assimilation policies, their collective voice cried for a return to their own customs of resolving conflict. In 1994, the Council of Neh-Kanikonriio (The Good Mind) was organized in Akwesasne, made up of about thirty men and women of all ages in the community.

The people looked at how the Way of Peace put priority on relationship rather than a structured hierarchy or punishments. Justice is defined as restoring a person to belonging. The indigenous system is about respecting elders and community values. European systems establish laws to obey. Native thought uses the condolence and offers counseling. European justice demands punishment. Restoration to victims and an honest admission of guilt differ from sentencing and punishment in American and Canadian courts. Court systems have adopted many of these restorative justice practices in recent years. There's new talk of collaboration between criminal and Native systems working with youth, providing cross-cultural training, establishing a liaison among police and government departments, installing custodial options, increasing elder involvement, and expanding community-based justice to restore offenders to their communities. The offenders first must give respect to Mother Earth, turning their thought to realize life's source and value. Then they must acknowledge what they have done. Everyone is asked for their recommendation to restore balance and restitution. Mirroring principles of the Great Law, offenders' clans come to them if they do something wrong and tell them to come back to the path. There may be a hardened youth charged with assault with a weapon, advised by his lawyer to come to this circle and find a safe place to cry. A non-Native victim can also seek solutions here to mend differences.

Structuring education to use it in their own way, the Haudenosaunee created the continent's first indigenous knowledge center, The Hiawatha Institute. The idea began in the 1990s when leaders met and determined to insure that the knowledge of the land's first peoples would continue. A board of nine directors formed on February 19, 2011. Committees created curriculum based on traditional teachings for programs partnered with Syracuse University. The institute fulfilled what began two hundred years ago as a vision of Shenandoah, an Oneida leader whose foresight envisioned a place where Native knowledge would be shared in a school of higher learning. There are ceremonies today held at the edges of the Haudenosaunee waters that bring together people from many communities, environmental groups, universities, and as far away as Japan. Prayer is said for the water's suffering and all the fish, turtles, and life within the lakes and rivers. Each person speaks in his or her own custom with the intent to help the waters be restored to health in a continuous cycle of replenishment. These words from diverse cultures are poured into the waters, and by them carried through the other territories and out to the salty ocean. There the sun lifts the water and the words into clouds for the wind to bring back as rain across the land.

When thunder rumbles in the air, the thunders are thanked as grandfathers. When there is a thunderstorm with loud claps of thunder and powerful lightening, an offering of tobacco is made to show thanks. Without the replenishing waters, earth would be in a drought. Life would cease. Without the thanks that acknowledge the gifts that hold life, the hollow sound of the black rattle could return, the way it did when the passenger pigeon went extinct, along with the wood bison and hundreds of Indian nations.

On winter days when daylight shortens and the sky lays heavy and cold over the land, the people hunker inside their houses for warmth. Many of the birds have migrated away. Gophers, chipmunks, frogs, and bats sleep. Beavers stay inside their dens with their stashes of foods. Weasels have on their winter white and black-tipped tails. The weeks are long. The people wait for the promise.

"The flowers appear on the earth; the time of singing of birds is come, and the voice of the turtle is heard in our land" (Song 2:12).

To bring the people out of their houses, gathering them together in a well-lit longhouse to share song and thanks and bring food to share with each other, the Haudenosaunee were given the Midwinter Ceremony.

The Mohawk begin with groups of roiane, elders, and little children walking through the community to carry a song to each house where they stir the old ashes of the fireplaces or wood stoves with a staff and prepare for a new fire.

At each house, they tell the families when the new year will begin, calculated by solstice, the following new moon and five nights. Then the ashes in the longhouse are stirred. The ashes drift into the air and sprinkle the earth, much the way seeds are covered at planting. The people also will be renewed in the new season.

The new fire means "we've committed to the responsibilities given by Creator for another year and we are thankful to Creator for continuing life cycles." Across the ocean in another land, the people of Judah were also given such festivals. Zechariah (Yahweh Remembers) said in 8:19: "The fasts of the fourth, fifth, seventh and tenth months will become joyful and glad occasions and happy festivals for Judah. Therefore love truth and peace."

Giving thanks moves people as part of the creation. The people recognize and celebrate the circle of the coming thunders, spring's new life, the Maple Ceremony, blessing seeds and planting, the growing season of the strawberry, green corn, and harvests, and preparing for winter cold. Deliverance, redemption, renewal, and protections are found in the essence of giving thanks, for each other, to all creation, to teachers sent to help us, and to Creator who gave us all life. If we've hurt anyone we've hurt Creator, because Creator is in them. After Haudenosaunee people struggled for the right to bring the ceremonies of their heritage into the prisons of New York, the giving of thanks continued inside those walls. Persons like Mohawk elder Tom Porter Sakokwenionkwas (The One Who Wins), hired by the state as a chaplain, explain to the prisoners that our lives are like a blackboard. It can get too many marks, then when someone comes to write on it, we can't read it. During Midwinter Ceremony a string of beads, a wampum, holds the fire, and can be looped over a finger and held to help a person release apologies and messages to Creator the way smoke is released with burning tobacco. The wampum helps to clear the board so Creator will see a person following the Great Peace. It must be renewed each year. This is the language of creation. Winter lingers in their lands until the frozen river cracks, allowing passage for a rivulet of water. The sun reaches down and touches deep into the earth and the water opens up, the flowers awaken with the people's prayers. The river dapples with light, released to flow again, the maple syrup comes, harvest will again be planted.

The sun's winds blow away yesterday with each new morning. "Because of the Lord's great love we are not consumed, for his compassions never fail. They are new every morning; great is your faithfulness" (Lam 3:22–23).

As both vessels turn focus to the river, they each want a healthy river, but the ship and canoe fight over jurisdiction. The ship looks at the river from a commercial perspective, changing standards every few decades and seeking only minimal protection. The canoe's view is about sustenance, following nature's unchanging standards. The poisons coming down on the people pressed MCA leaders on the north shores of the reserve in 1976 to start the Indians' first Department of Environment. On the south shores there came a need for an environmental department to address the federal Superfund and two state Superfund sites next to the reservation. As MCA's department worked on the north shores of the St. Lawrence River, the SRMT established their Environmental Health Division on the south shores in 1980, with a workforce of about eighteen community members monitoring air, education, land, water, and restoration. Because of the political and jurisdictional quagmire, leaders decided to create a task force that could provide a way for all the environmental organizations on the reserve to come together for what they all agreed on—understanding the impacts of contamination, getting the information to the community, and working on a way to clean the river.

So in 1987 community volunteers formed the Akwesasne Task Force on Environment. When we hear of land and governance disputes, what the people are talking about is not rights. It is responsibility that is inherent in a way of life. All elements are entwined and all feel the impacts when forces act to disrupt healthy relationships. So when the Mohawk talk about, for instance, diabetes, they see the whole, from the cellular system to the individual to the spiritual. They don't just treat the individual. They treat the family, for example by encouraging gardening. The family is in the community, so a step up the scale of levels is community gardening. In looking at diabetes the Mohawk model has about fifty components that they see affecting the disease, compared to American, Canadian, and European models that contain eighteen. To be healthy and live in a good way is more than the absence of disease. It includes the presence of all the elements of spiritual, physical, and social health. The Mohawk worked with the University of Ottawa on the problems afflicting many northern communities and created health indicators. They turned to elders who had spent time with children, telling stories, planting, cooking, passing along ancestral knowledge of people and places. Elders drew a circle and called it "health," dividing it into segments that look like a pie chart with, for example, picnics and community gatherings in one segment (the sociological), and sunlight in another (the environmental). This approach would examine a depressed community and instead of the Western response that would say "needs economic development and jobs," it would consider both biology and abuse going on within a community. The population of moose falls, for instance, and men believe they are bad hunters, unable to provide for their families. They stop trying, go on welfare, and begin to drink. Their wives no longer have the work of preparing the moose. Sons no longer have pride in going out with the men. Abuse and crime go up. The solution is not more jobs. It's in the moose population. When the population becomes healthy, the hunters are successful again and the family success is restored. When they sensed a lack of spirituality, communities made more water drums. Western science was studying people and telling them they're not healthy. Western knowledge is useful information but it brings no hope. The circle segments bring to view the imbalance, what is missing. People are given hope. They are empowered to see what is needed to restore their own health.

The premise of a good mind generates a circle of respect, equity, and empowerment. When we come to know our connection to the living world, we begin to know our role in it. Then the circle brings meaning for us.

"These all look to you to give them their food at the proper time. When you give it to them, they gather it up; when you open your hand, they are satisfied with good things. When you hide your face, they are terrified; when you take away their breath, they die and return to the dust. When you send your Spirit, they are created, and you renew the face of the earth" (Ps 104:27–30).

When the world was made and people were given this relationship it extended to elder brother, the sun. Every day he brings light, lingering high at noon, pouring light over what we're doing on earth.

Elder brother's rays intensified with global warming. Long before talk of global warming, Indian prophecy said the ground would be so hot in places that birds couldn't land. Recently, the life-giving star set the lowest records for sunspots, weak solar wind, and low solar irradiance in the last century. The eleven-year cycles of the five-billion-year-old star have lasted well beyond the year 2007, when scientists predicted it would charge up again. The star is waking up now, churning solar storms, readying to blast sky weather, erupting waves that rip through space, reaching earth in a few minutes, casting up its plumes of fire to transfer into earthquakes that open the ground and swallow the people, feeding the serpent beneath the ground. Solar winds speed off the sun, vibrating with electrically charged atoms flowing at more than 500,000 miles per hour, burning cancers into living beings as ozone protections disappear. Some forecast geomagnetic storms that will threaten electrical grids around the world, causing up to $2 million in damages to high-tech infrastructure.

It's all our situation now. In July 2013, four centuries after the first treaty was woven with non-Natives, the Two-Row Wampum, a hundred Natives and non-Natives paddled side by side from Onondaga to Albany to the Hudson River to New York City. Then, on August 9, they walked across Manhattan to the UN for the International Day of the World's Indigenous Peoples. The sojourn, called the Two-Row Wampum Renewal Campaign, took about two weeks. A replica of the wampum was presented to Rob de Vos, Consul General at the Netherlands Consulate General in New York City. "We can learn so much from you and especially we can learn from you how to live with nature, with our earth," he said. "We all realize today we have to protect ourselves."

The next day the forum held a gathering, Honor the Two-Row. Faithkeeper Oren Lyons spoke. "The question is how do you instruct seven billion people as to their relationship to earth, because only if we respect and understand our relationships will we as a species survive." It's a shift in global awareness, with people of all sorts now wanting to come together to preserve the future of children yet to be born, and to understand the dichotomy between Native and non-Native peoples.

This came after centuries of leaders traveling to Washington, DC, and finding no understanding among the non-Native population. The well-being of the water had begun bringing them together. Tagged along the journey were stickers saying "Honor Native Treaties to Protect the Earth." Landscape everywhere has seen changes pushed by a faster pace.

Heavy traffic now drives into Jerusalem, a city sprawling with 750,000 people. Green cedars and slender trees grow from rocky soil. Construction and scaffolding cross the horizon. Many denominations of Christian churches have set up around Jerusalem. Travelers must carry all the correct documents. A wall stretches many miles, separating the West Bank from Israel like a high prison wall, topped with razor wire and guard encased in bulletproof glass, armed with search lights and electronic sensing devices. Soldiers stand with M16 submachine guns hanging from straps around their shoulders. The wall is intended to exclude the Palestinians. From the Mount of Olives, which holds the sacred site of the garden of Gethsemane, the place of the walled city built by King David three thousand years ago can be seen. Jesus would have looked out onto this.

Israelites wait for the temple to be rebuilt. The first temple built by Solomon was destroyed by Nebuchadnezzar, and rebuilt when the Jews returned from exile in what is now Iraq. This second temple was torn down by Romans around 100 AD, but the Western Wall, called HaKotel, still stands, sacred to the people. Two-thousand-year-old olive trees grow in the garden of Gethsemane where Jesus went to pray. This is where Jesus was betrayed and dragged along a rugged, steep slope to the court at Mt. Zion before being taken to Pontius Pilot's court, east of the Dome of the Rock built in 690 AD.

Today Bedouin Arabs camp in the hills with herds of goats scavenging for vegetation on a hot dry land. Orchards of palms grow near the Dead Sea's shores, a rapidly shrinking sea forty-five miles long and a few miles wide. Companies set up on the shore to extract its minerals, much of it for cosmetics.

The Jordan River flows into the Dead Sea, some 1,200 miles below sea level, the lowest place on earth. Jesus must have hiked the long thirsty trail from Nazareth to be baptized in the Jordan River. It's now a smuggling route for contraband from Jordan to Israel and is heavily patrolled at night. Access to the oldest continually inhabited city on earth, Jericho, is controlled by Palestinian police.

Tensions build around the world. Every treaty made has been broken. Not one has been kept. At the end times, it will be the breaking of a covenant with Israel, a seven-year treaty, that will signal the coming great tribulation, a time of horror the world has never seen. There will be a small band of God's people who persevere.

In 1992, the Royal Commission on Aboriginal Peoples, to find ways to restore justice to relationship between Aboriginal and non-Aboriginal people in Canada, appointed four Aboriginal and three non-Aboriginal commissioners. Their report stated:

It was a time of anger and upheaval. The country's leaders were arguing about the place of Aboriginal people in the constitution. First Nations were blockading roads and rail lines in Ontario and British Columbia. Innu families were encamped in protest of military installations in Labrador. A year earlier, armed conflict between Aboriginal and non-Aboriginal forces at Kanesatake (Oka) had tarnished Canada's reputation abroad—and in the minds of many citizens. It was a time of concern and distress. Media reports had given Canadians new reasons to be disturbed about the facts of life in many Aboriginal communities: high rates of poverty, ill health, family break-down and suicide. Children and youth were most at risk. It was also a time of hope. Aboriginal people were rebuilding their ancient ties to one another and searching their cultural heritage for the roots of their identity and the inspiration to solve community problems.

They held 178 days of public hearings, visited ninety-six communities, consulted dozens of experts, commissioned research, and reviewed reports. Their final recommendation was to return to the treaties. "In our minds, if we are looking toward a future where we can have peace in this land, the mechanism is there, and that is . . . those relationships of friendship. . . . That is the foundation we have to begin with," said Charlie Otsi'tsaken:ra Patton, Bear Clan, Mohawk roiane of the traditional council.

5

Women

May our sons in their youth be like plants full grown, our daughters like corner pillars cut for the structure of a palace.

PSALM 144:12

AN ESTIMATED 70,000 NATIVE women were sterilized without their knowledge by the US government during the 1970s. The procedures were performed by the Indian Health Service without their consent, with language barriers, and under threats that they would lose their welfare benefits if they birthed another child. In some cases, teenage girls came in to have their tonsils removed and left with their ovaries removed.

The documents were publicized by Native women during the civil rights movements, among them Katsi Cook, a Mohawk from Akwesasne. She began working in her community to restore women's bodies to balance with the rhythms of earth and sky. A birthing crew was established in 1980 through the Women's Dance Health Program and began recovering the act of birth and trust in traditional ways.

Water is our first environment, in the womb where a child forms. In women is a core definition of sovereignty—the right to raise children in their own heritage.

The women wondered if the toxins in the river were making their way into mothers' breast milk. When industries were built along the St.

Lawrence River, poisons began pouring into the ancient river. Unknown to the Mohawk people downriver, more than 297,000 tons of PCBs and other poisons settled quietly into the river sediment and on vegetation eaten by fish and wildlife that made their way into the food chain. PAHs, dioxins, dibenzofurans, metals, cyanide, mercury, mirex, and styrene were discharged into the air, land, and water around the Mohawk people. Companies discharged PCBs until the EPA ban in 1978.

Fish moved about beneath the water, swallowing smaller fish, absorbing the poisons, building it up in their fatty tissues, to be eaten by larger fish, birds, and people. Or they sank to the bottom when they died, to be eaten by invertebrates who are eaten by fish, recycling the toxins for years, damaging eyes, nervous systems, reproductive systems, livers, thyroids, and kidneys, and fueling cancerous growth throughout the web of food.

The women gathered to talk. From those meetings, in October 1999 the First Environmental Research Project was established to learn about the effects of the toxins in utero and in newborn children. Later it grew to examine the impact on the thyroids and behavior of adolescents, through a study in partnership with universities and the National Institute of Environmental Health Sciences. PCBs among 115 young adults of Akwesasne were studied. Eighteen, 15.4 percent, had antithyroid peroxidase antibody levels above the normal range. PCB was significantly higher among those who were breast fed.

Americans are taught that their country was built on prayer as the first Congress knelt to ask God's blessing. So, for instance, the Liberty Bell was engraved in 1752 with "Proclaim liberty throughout all the land unto all the inhabitants thereof" (Lev 25:10). American societies grew. Churches were built. But for the original peoples, the history of the church began with murder, enslavement, and punishments, sundering relationship with home, land, and family. Generations who heard the sound of a knock on the door still think of Indian Agents there to take away the children. We call Washington one of our founders. The Haudenosaunee call him Hanadagayus, Village Burner.

In the middle of the Revolution, in 1779, General Washington ordered Generals John Sullivan and James Clinton to slaughter the Six Nations. Writing to General Gates, Washington said, "It is proposed to carry the war into the country of the Six Nations, to cut off their settlements, destroy their next year's crops and do them every other mischief which time and circumstances will permit." He ordered, "the immediate objects are the total destruction of their settlements and the capture of as many prisoners of every sex and age as possible. It is essential to ruin their crops in the ground and prevent their planting." General Sullivan was to "Lay waste all the settlements around, so that the country might not only be overrun, but destroyed."

More than six thousand men of the rebel army entered Indian country in Pennsylvania as the season ripened a harvest. They marched to the eastern shores of Seneca Lake, down the western shores of Cayuga Lake, then up the eastern side. As they went, they destroyed whole fields of crops, burning and throwing hundreds of thousands of bushels of corn into the lake, axing down hundreds of trees loaded with ripe fruits.

The first raid lasted five days in April, then came another in the four weeks of September. Sullivan's official report said the army burned more than five hundred homes in more than forty towns "with a vast quantity of vegetables of every kind." Clinton wrote, "Defenceless women and children, the aged grandaire and the sturdy youth, oft fell in one promiscuous slaughter."

After the Sullivan Campaign, Governor George Clinton began patching up the relationship with the Haudenosaunee at a council at Fort Stanwix in April 1784. Clinton said: "We have no Claim on your Lands: its just extent will ever remain secured to you." Then they proceeded to pay missionaries who were also being paid by developers to remove the Six Nations to make way for the Erie Canal.

Five centuries of oppressions committed in the name of Jesus caused many hearts to harden toward the name of Christ. The way the residential schools, removal policies, and forced adoptions used the name of Jesus left many angry about white man's religion, confused about a savior who would promote such violent ripping apart of families, deceitful taking away of lands, forced assimilation from natural heritage, and punishments and fear. And still our God waits to be known.

When creation was forming, Wisdom was present, delighting in God's plan: "When there were no oceans, I was given birth, when there were no springs abounding with water . . . when he set the heavens in place, when he marked out the horizon on the face of the deep, when he established the clouds above and fixed securely the fountains of the deep, when he gave the sea its boundary so the waters would not overstep his command, and when he marked out the foundations of the earth, then I was the craftsman at his side" (Prov 8:24). Wisdom is personified as female. She encourages, "blessed are those who keep my ways" (Prov 8:22).

Creation stories around the world tend to use the feminine when talking about life's continuance, while the structure of protocols and laws that enable relationship tend to be masculine. In the Haudenosaunee creation story the peopling of earth began when Sky Woman fell from the sky world. A tree grows in the middle of the sky world called the tree of life, with blossoms that produce many kinds of seeds. The tree was not to be disturbed but one day Atsi'tsiaka:ion, who was pregnant, asked her husband for tea made from the roots of the tree. As her husband dug, dirt caved in and there was a hole. Atsi'tsiaka:ion, referred to as Sky Woman, went through the hole, grabbing seeds from the tree of life as she fell toward earth. Deep waters covered earth. As Atsi'tsiaka:ion fell through the sky a flock of birds caught her on their backs and helped her to land upon a turtle. As she waited for the animals to bring up earth to increase the space on turtle's shell, Atsi'tsiaka:ion marked time by marking the turtle's back with twenty-eight sections around the edge and thirteen sections in the middle of the shell. These became the people's annual 364-day calendar (13 x 28 = 364).

One of the animals at last dove deep enough and brought up earth from beneath the water, placing it upon the turtle to become a continent known as Turtle Island. Atsi'tsiaka:ion, lost from all she had known, accepted her destiny toward a new creation and danced counterclockwise around the earth on turtle's back, singing songs she brought from the other world. As she moved, the earth expanded and stretched as far as she could see. She planted the seeds for strawberries and tobacco from her world to help the people live well.

When she died she was buried in the earth. From the body of earth the seeds grew. Beans grew. Squash grew. Rising from the heart were strawberries. Then came corn. Tobacco symbolizes a good path in life and grew to help the people talk with Creator. The radiance of Grandmother Moon remains in the sky as her face watches through the generations. Her twenty-eight-day cycles mark the cycle of a woman's body and remind women of their connection to the life-giving earth of Turtle Island. The season's first fruit, strawberry, recalls the gift from the sky world. This is celebrated each spring as a new cycle of life begins. Its scent leads along the Milky Way as a person who dies returns to the place of the sky world. Honoring these gifts of life, the Haudenosaunee dances move in the counterclockwise direction the way Sky Woman danced. Other peoples such as the Ojibwe move around the fire and dance clockwise as was given to them on the land where they live. The different peoples that God appointed to live on the North

American continent respected each other's ways of acknowledging the one Creator with their respective traditions of giving thanks. They did not try to convert each other. No one born Mohawk could become Dine' any more than someone born English could become part of the Jewish lineage. These traditions teach that gifts come with responsibilities that each people, each plant, bird, fish, and animal were given. "How many are your works, O Lord! In wisdom you made them all; the earth is full of your creatures" (Ps 104:24).

The Lord finds us by not only accepting who we are but valuing us for it, and we become aware that it was he who created us. Those who stood for their heritage made it possible for the first people's children to today retain their language and the stories of their ancestry that teach them ways of compassion and living on the land.

But trusted bonds broken by a church system have resulted in inabilities to parent and provide this stability. The increase in single-parent families and children being raised by grandparents denote a break with the role of women. When Peacemaker stepped onto the shores he entered a time when women were afraid of their own men. Accepting his message of governance was a woman of the Neutral Nation called Jikonsahseh, sometimes translated as Beautiful Countenance. Jikonsahseh had a camp in Seneca lands at the crossroads of warpaths. She is said to have told the men to leave their weapons outside before entering to refresh themselves. Yet she encouraged their fighting and instigated trouble between them—until she heard the message of the Peacemaker. After meeting him she advocated unity for everyone she met and she is often referred to as a mother to the Six Nations. The walls of her camp are still visible, grown over now in an orchard, a place in the history of their formation as a league that brought the people out of war. All over the Americas are sites meaningful to the original people that tell stories about how they are part of the land. 300 years ago, Ganondagan, located southeast of Rochester, was the site of a vibrant Seneca village where Jikonsaheh is said to be buried. In 1980 Peter Jemison, a faithkeeper of the Seneca Nation, was hired as site manager of a museum and teaching center through the Division of Historic Preservation. Nine years later the Friends of Ganondagan incorporated under the state education law to bring about education and promote the message of peace.

There can be no functioning longhouse without the iakoia:ne (clan mother), roiane (chief), and two faithkeepers: male (roterihonton) and female (iaterihonton). There is also an advisor. All must work in concert on behalf of their clans and community. The four insure no one person has too much authority, that there is a creative energy for ideas to be exchanged and keep the leadership balanced.

Faithkeepers not only serve as ceremonial leaders but act as political advisors to the clan mothers and roiane. They have to make sure all the collective rituals are conducted in the proper manner and will sit with the roiane and clan mothers during these events. Theirs is the task of watching the movements of the natural world and advising the people as to when they should gather to plant, give thanks, and hold meetings. They are teachers of great influence since they carry the customs to the next generation. Leadership promotes trust in God's intent for our well-being. However much the world can break our lives and minds, it can never break our ability to speak with our Creator. "For the mountains may depart and the hills be removed, but my steadfast love shall not depart from you, and my covenant of peace shall not be removed, says the Lord, who has compassion on you" (Isa 54:10).

Peacemaker gave the women authority to nominate the roiane in each of the Confederacy's nations after they counsel with all in their clan. The women watch as a child grows, know his character, his strengths and weaknesses. They recognize leadership that can be trusted. At the same time, the children are absorbing the lessons of the women. They are being taught all day, introduced to the sun, the plants, the water, taught to say Nia:wen (thank you) to Creator for all these things that make life possible. Spirituality suffuses every part of the day. Shell strings of wampum are given to each of the clan mothers, bestowing this right to sponsor a leader from her clan and the responsibility of bringing him back into balance with the council if he goes off in a wrong way. Mohawk have three clans—bear, wolf and turtle. Each clan has these five leadership positions, with their holders serving for life. "Older women likewise are to be reverent in behavior, not slanderers or slaves to much wine. They are to teach what is good, and so train the young women to love their husbands and children." (Titus 2:3-4). Family lineage passes through the female clan as it does with the Hebrew people under talmudic law. A child belongs to the clan of the mother. In the Great Way Wampum, "The women of every clan in the Hotinonshonni shall have a continuous Council Fire burning for the purpose of holding a Council meeting of that clan when it is necessary in the interest of the people."

Peacemaker saw how women are out among the families, talking to each other. They hear about the needs. They know when resources are insufficient or when someone is distraught. They gather together to plant gardens or weave baskets, today to form health care systems and to create programs for birthing, for language, and for teaching. Peacemaker understood the people's movement with the seasons, the guidance of the moon in the female cycles of birth. The governance he brought structured a way for the women to bring these concerns to the roiane as decisions are made responding from the heart of a community.

We and those around us need to be clear minded, centered in the Spirit of God. Just as the flock of birds caught Atsi'tsiaka:ion in the air, we catch each other if we fall and help one another to land on solid ground.

The 2010 meeting at the UN asking for a study of the misuse of Christ as a rationale to dominate other peoples signaled a historic shift. Non-Natives begin to see their own reflections, redefining their identity as Christians. Natives question the true meaning of Christianity.

Murray Sinclair, Chairperson of the Truth and Reconciliation Commission of Canada, talked about how the first nations had not assimilated despite 150 years of racist policies. While there's damage, the cultures and languages are very much there. What their stories tell us is that their need is to become who they are before true relationship can come about with the non-Natives living beside them. Their strength is in being rooted individually. Relationship is in the branches that grow from communal roots.

Ellen Gabriel, Femmes Autochtones du Quebec, speaking at the UN's Permanent Forum, said Canada's refusal to embark on a postcolonial process had hindered women's full participation in decision-making processes. Education systems are improving awareness. In America classrooms highlight the First Amendment of the Constitution, emphasizing how religious liberty places on all people a responsibility to protect that right for others. The First Amendment states, "Congress shall make no law respecting an establishment of religion, or prohibiting the free exercise thereof," understanding that no one should be made to worship against their own conscience. The Native people call on towns and governments to follow their laws of justice. It is a voice calling for America to heal.

Biblically, the first lie spoken in the creation was said to a woman, confusing her identity by telling her she could have fulfillment outside God's design. Echoing this theme, native people say, "If you want to destroy a country all it takes is for the women's hearts to be on the ground." This enmity would manifest by targeting women everywhere on earth with degradation, separation, abuse, lies, loneliness, violence, and male domination. The little girl who was never hugged and protected. The mother who heard only belittling words if she spoke her thoughts. The young women raped. The young women sold to perverse men, trapped with no way to survive. Or led down to the pit by society's messages devaluing her. Grandmothers helpless to reach out to their children's children. Or women bruised and broken, terrified of fleeing an abusive husband. Those so empty they fume with jealousy and gossip. The ones betrayed by cheating husbands, then themselves becoming adulterers in response. The desolate and despairing.

Suicide rates increased most among American Indian and Alaska Natives, 2.5 percent higher than the national average, according to the Center for Disease Control, with rates now surging among the middle aged. Risk factors for women include abandonment, sexual abuse, violence, and abortion, that leave them to the stark realization that their lives are not centered in being loved and supported enough to celebrate new life. Native women today aged twenty-five to forty-four are five times more likely than other women to die from violence, according to Amnesty International. In Canada 582 cases of missing or murdered Native women and girls were reported in 2013. Many were mothers. An estimated eighty-eight percent left behind children and grandchildren. Native children have become overrepresented in the child welfare system.

This is what was brought to the people here. It caused a stress on today's community equal to the aftermath of an earthquake. Now reflecting our standards onto ourselves, we question how to bring better fruit as the people come together to release a new future. All these losses, these atrocities and injustices occurred.

Response does not yield easily to a force that has caused such debilitation, but we were given a universal answer in when the serpent in the garden of Eden tempted the woman away from God's instructions. God spoke to the serpent: "And I will put enmity between you and the woman, and between your offspring and hers; he will crush your head, and you will strike his heel" (Gen 3:15).

If tearing apart by attacking is the serpent's ploy, then giving thanks for God and all that he provides is the balance. When God spoke to the serpent, his words gave women individually and collectively the power to carry the joy of God's mercies even in times of distress The story of Deborah in the book of Judges illustrates how one woman's encouragement to men to believe God defeated the people's enemy. Deborah was among the men and women who God raised to act as judges to lead the way out of oppressions. The children of Israel had fallen away from listening to their instructions and had been sold into Canaan, where they cried out to God for help, sorry now that they had not listened.

For twenty years they lived under the hand of King Jabin. Deborah spoke with Barak, a military leader, asking him to lead an attack against the Canaanite armies. She prophesied that Sisera, a man who murdered and raped women among those he called enemies, would be killed by a woman. During battle the Canaanite chariots got stuck in mire when wind carried in clouds bursting with enough rain to flood the river. Sisera fled to a Jael's tent, where the Hebrew woman killed him by pounding his head with a tent peg. King Jabin fled and the people were liberated. Then sang Deborah and Barak the son of Abinoam on that day,

> In the days of Shamgar son of Anath,
> in the days of Jael, the highways were abandoned;
> travelers took to winding paths.
> Villagers in Israel would not fight;
> they held back until I, Deborah, arose,
> until I arose, a mother in Israel.
> God chose new leaders

when war came to the city gates,
but not a shield or spear was seen
among forty thousand in Israel.
My heart is with Israel's princes,
with the willing volunteers among the people.
Praise the LORD! (Judg 5:6–9)

The Jewish people lived peacefully as a new generation grew up during the next twenty years. In North America the Native Women's Association of Canada (NWAC) formed in 1974, struggling to shed light on the inequalities experienced by Aboriginal women and girls, caused by colonial policies that broke apart family and community, leaving them vulnerable to violence and trauma. The call for others to join NWAC's concerns was made at a 2003 gathering of Canadian churches in Ottawa. In the spirit of the Two-Row Wampum the United Church of Canada and the Anglican Church joined to launch Sisters in Spirit, a campaign for research and education ending oppressions through shared celebration for the gifts God has given to women.

It is an example reflected in what Paul explained: "Carry each other's burdens," and "each one should carry their own load" (Gal 6:2, 6). Letters and phone calls were made to the government for funding for Sisters in Spirit. Strategies formed, and awareness raised to reduce violence against Native women. Vigils were held in nearlytwo hundred places across the United States and Canada on October 4. Rallies, candle-lit memorials, workshops, moments of silence, walks, or gatherings for meals, all enacted for social change, have brought increased understanding that what is most needed to prevent social problems is a return to knowledge of women's role in community. The strength carried by rejoicing in Mohawk land is expressed in the ceremonial dances giving thanks, the friendship dance with other nations, and the traditional dances the young are learning to carry on. The beat of the water drum, the sound of the singers' voices, continued through centuries of the heaviest oppressions, brings minds into a celebration of the unchanging promise of Creator. The sound lifts to the sky over the people, keeping them in the presence of God when they most need help to hold on to the strengths. The notes fall low, bringing people back to the earth we stand upon.

As missionaries established themselves among the Mohawk people, they condemned anyone who practiced their culture with threats of a punishing God. They mocked their beliefs and thanksgiving as superstition.

But there were people who continued it, sometimes having to leave for Onondaga, the Grand River, or the Seneca community to attend seasonal ceremonies. Ceremonies were nearly extinguished by the 1920s but persevered through the policies. Now again these gatherings move with the cycle of the coming thunders, spring's new life, the Maple Ceremony, the blessing of seeds and planting, the growing season of the strawberry, thanksgiving for green corn and harvests, preparing for winter, and commemorating the midwinter. All of these ceremonies ask for another cycle of life. It is not the worship of creation, as early newcomers so often scoffed. It is a thanksgiving for each other and each member of creation for collectively serving God as workers who keep life continuing for us all. It is a thanksgiving to the mystery that is God for putting all this in place. It is respect for a Father's garden left in their hands for care. The Apostle Paul wrote, "The heavens declare the glory of God; the skies proclaim the work of his hands. Day after day they pour forth speech; night after night they display knowledge. There is no speech or language where their voice is not heard. Their voice goes out into all the earth, their words to the ends of the world" (Rom 1:19–20).

When the snow melts around the base of the tree, the Maple Ceremony begins with the run of sap and ratihsesta:tas (putting in the sap). The thanksgiving before planting season comes again. The people gather together at the longhouse. A speaker burns tobacco, giving thanks for trees and bushes, especially the maple tree for coming out of winter sleep to bring maple syrup. Prayer asks that the young men be kept safe as they tap the trees. Soon smoke is rising from a sugar shack and everyone will have syrup. The Strawberry Ceremony occurs when the wild strawberries ripen and acknowledges the promise from Creator to continue life. The Green Corn Ceremony brings thanks when the corn's ears are ready to be boiled or roasted. The ceremony celebrates a season of abundance. The Harvest Ceremony gives gratitude for the Three Sisters and the foods earth provides. The Midwinter Ceremony's games and dances fill the longhouse with community during the dark cold days of the land's long winter, in faith for the coming spring. The midwinter days unfold with the voices of the Wolf Clan men singing the dawn song. A group of women follow to each house to bring women into the Women's Dance to honor Our Life Sustainers—the Three Sisters. The males give thanks to Creator for their families. A successful hunt is celebrated. In the afternoon, the people prepare for the Big Feather Dance, when the people dance with all of creation to honor the Creator and give thanks for the gifts of life. It reflects Psalm 148, spoken to another people and telling them that all creation is with us in our giving of thanks: "Praise the Lord from the earth, you great sea creatures and all ocean depths, lightning and hail, snow and clouds, stormy winds that do his bidding, you mountains and all hills, fruit trees and all cedars, wild animals and all cattle, small creatures and flying birds, kings of the earth and all nations, you princes and all rulers on earth, young men and maidens, old men and children."

Clan mothers give newborn babies their Indian names at this time. During the Mohawk Naming Ceremony it's said that every person has a gift. All children come here bringing something. Their elders watch as the child grows to discover his or her strength. What can this child do? It may be art or teaching, or maybe he's a great speaker or singer or lacrosse player. The Seven Dances of the women to honor women and Mother Earth are performed in the evening. These thanksgivings have continued to flow out across the lands here for thousands of years, carried in the water, through the trees reaching to sky, and to each other. "For by him all things were created: things in heaven and on earth, visible and invisible, whether thrones or powers or rulers or authorities; all things were created by him and for him" (Col 1:16–17).

Peacemaker, Hiawatha, and Jikonsahseh insured that the gift of women is vested to help the people survive what would be wave after wave of sorrows, violence, epidemics, disruption, forced removal of their little ones, and the taking and poisoning of lands and waters that had sustained their generations.

The East filled with missionaries telling the people that they're not living right, not praying to their God in the way they should. The cultures of the Anglo-Saxons absorbed Christianity into their own formalities, a pyramid placing power with one man on top, a system depending on growing its population and pushing down any other group. Catholicism, Lutheranism, and Calvinism were making Europe a hotbed of disunity. People fled and sought refuge when Protestants were under threat from Queen Mary I. Religion rolled across the tribal peoples of Europe, the Alemanni, Goths, Gauls, Magyars, Huns, Vandals, and Franks, with tactics deployed by the Roman Empire. In fifteenth-century Ireland, the Doctrine of Discovery made Henry VIII decide to forbid the people from wearing their traditional Celtic clothing in an attempt to destroy their sense of unity. Irish women covered their heads with linen but didn't wear corsets like the English. Young girls let their hair flow long and loose. Men braided their long hair, a custom punished by the Anglo-Saxons. For two centuries the Protestant and Catholic churches took in an estimated 30,000 Irish women, held at Magdalene asylums throughout Ireland, until the last closed in 1996. They were intended to rehabilitate fallen women as well young girls who had been raped and considered unclean, or any female a male of the household decided to bring into line. These women would find themselves in the prisonlike wards under enforced prayer, silence, little education, and long periods of hard labor and laundry duties for hospitals and businesses.

One of the things missionaries found most disturbing in North America was the autonomy of the women. They saw how the women spoke for the nation. They saw how the people's supplies and the protocols of ceremonies were nurtured by the women. They learned that the extensive gardens and orchards, lands, and children were within the domain of the women. Missionary wives witnessed how the clan mothers worked with the roiane who were the spokespeople.

Living side by side with the women of the Six Nations, they witnessed the equally shared responsibilities of the Haudenosaunee women. Among them were Matilda Joslyn Gage (1826–1898), Elizabeth Cady Stanton (1815–1902), and Lucretia Mott (1793–1880), all living in the oppressed age when even discussion of marital rape was outlawed by Comstock laws and the church upheld that women, once married, were dead in the law. The mother gave birth to the child but had no right to the child. The husband had not only the right, but the responsibility to chastise a woman. The Supreme Court at the time said he did not break the law by beating her and that to interfere would "upset the domestic tranquility of the home."

Elizabeth and Matilda coauthored the Declaration of Rights of the Women of the United States, presented at the Centennial celebration by Matilda and Susan Anthony in Washington in 1876. Matilda, who served as president of the National Woman Suffrage Association in 1875, said the "division of power between the sexes in its Indian republic was nearly equal."

It's not about having power. It's about balance and the equal value of each gender's responsibilities. Mohawk notions of gender differences are based on different roles and different work, not on being the same. It's about shared responsibilities that will keep the family, the clan, the community, the nation, and the Confederacy well.

Women birth children, men go out hunting, and everyone takes care of the children and gardens and puts food away for the future. In tradition, women are not to cook for a ceremony if angry or grieving because the influence of emotion has importance.

When the early white women saw all this they were sparked with vision that gave them courage. It wasn't just about women's rights. There was a food reform movement for eating whole grains and vegetables, and to learn the medicinal plants to heal from illness.

Scripture says "the earth is the Lord's and everything in it, the world, and all who live in it; for he founded it upon the seas and established it upon the waters" (Ps 24:1–2), and that "By faith we understand that the universe was formed at God's command, so that what is seen was not made out of what was visible" (Heb 11:3).

A balance was given. Grandmother Moon governed the female cycles of regeneration in relationship with the water. The rising and setting of our Brother the Sun is male time. The sun leads the way across the sky to provide structure to the day, an eldest brother that men follow in their responsibilities to provide fire for their family's warmth and gathering to learn the teachings. The fire burns when councils meet to make decisions, its smoke rising as prayer toward heaven.

As scientists suggest the surface of the moon is shrinking and the quiet sun is readying to erupt into solar storms, humans on earth have come to organize an economic structure in which made it so that, by 2008, of the hundred dominant economic units in the world, forty-nine were countries and fifty-one were corporations. After endorsing the UN Declaration on the Rights of Indigenous Peoples, the Obama administration did not entirely accept the clause "free, prior and informed consent" that would give indigenous peoples a say in vetoing plans of corporate development in or near their territories.

The St. Lawrence River had suffered under toxins. The delta of Nigeria suffered under the Shell Oil Company. Mining in West Papua, nuclear waste in Yakama homeland, hydrofracking being opposed near Haudenosaunee territories, all continued after the 1983 policy affirming government-to-government relationship with Indian nations, Alaskan Natives, and Hawaiian Natives.

Not finding justice, during the twelfth session of the UN Permanent Forum on Indigenous Issues on May 28, 2013, seventy-two American Indian and Alaskan Native nations signed a joint statement calling for the UN to facilitate discussions at an international level. All our achievements have not healed fallen humanity. For every effort to fix a problem more problems are created along with the potential to destroy what was being fixed. The stars cradle earth in a celestial tree of life, our Creator sings over us, and yet the original curse continues.

"We know that the whole creation has been groaning as in the pains of childbirth right up to the present time" (Rom 8:22). "The creation waits in eager expectation for the sons of God to be revealed. For the creation was subjected to frustration, not by its own choice, but by the will of the one who subjected it, in hope that the creation itself will be liberated from its bondage to decay and brought into the glorious freedom of the children of God" (Rom 8:19-21).

We are the seeds, needing to die to self and send roots reaching to his water, needing growth to become the flowering resource that sustains many lives with God's sweet fragrance, without our preconceived ideas of what God should do. The cause of all mistaken choices, separations, and the history that tried to plant all one kind of plant is in the unbelief in the diversity and equality that Jesus intends.

There will be a day when these divisions and differences will resolve. No one will suffer. No one will feel scared of another person. That time begins when Jesus returns.

Then the lion will lay down with the lamb. No longer will they be under the rule that makes animals hunt each other. The deer and the wolf will again be friends.

Until then we continue with the struggles of learning from each other, trusting each other, and facing the coming future together. As we fulfill each of our assignments we come closer and make the path ready for those behind us.ABraham, Paul, Jeremiah, Jesus, Peacemaker, and the many unknown who worked steadily in their communities, worked to make the path ready. All moved under the guidance of the same Spirit and made sacrifices in which they found their fulfillment. They loved the eternal song of heaven more than the transient gains on earth. They brought fragrance to each broken life, to make these lives part of God's meadow.

Solomon's song refers to Christ's redeemed as among the lilies, and sings, "The voice of my beloved! Look, he comes, leaping upon the mountains, bounding over the hills. . . . My lover is mine and I am his; he browses among the lilies." The song continues, "My beloved has gone down to his garden, to the beds of spices, to pasture his flock in the gardens, and to gather lilies. I am my beloved's and my beloved is mine; he pastures his flock among the lilies" (Song 2, 6).

Hosea 14:7 reinforces this theme that our lives are made part of God's meadow: "They shall again live beneath my shadow, they shall flourish as a garden; they shall blossom like the vine, their fragrance shall be like the wine of Lebanon." So does Luke 12:27: "Observe the lilies, how they grow. They neither labor nor spin. And yet I tell you that not even Solomon in all his splendor was as beautifully dressed as one of these." So, again, does Jeremiah 31:12: "They will be like a well-watered garden, and they will sorrow no more." In this spirit 2 Corinthians 2:14–15 reads, "But thanks be to God, who always leads us in triumphal procession in Christ and through us spreads everywhere the fragrance of the knowledge of him. For we are to God the aroma of Christ." This description of taking on the beauty and fragrance of Christ is mirrored in the sanctity of female and male union. "I promised you to one husband, to Christ, so that I might present you as a pure virgin to him. But I am afraid that just as Eve was deceived by the serpent's cunning, your minds may somehow be led astray from your sincere and pure devotion to Christ" (2 Cor 11:2–3).

The twelfth chapter of the Revelation tells us there will be a company of perfected believers with Christ, indebted to the female who is the life giver. "A great sign appeared in heaven: a woman clothed with the sun, with the moon under her feet, and on her head a crown of twelve stars. She was pregnant and cried out in pain as she was about to give birth" (Rev 12:1–2).

These are believers, persecuted, escaping to the wilderness. Satan will follow to war against "the rest of her offspring—those who obey God's commandments and hold to the testimony of Jesus" (Rev 15:17).

Jesus suggested this time would come like birth pangs, intermittently at first, intensifying until the flood of water, his Holy Spirit, brought the new creation from the seed of his word. One of the phenomena of the natural world is how a star grows to its brightest just before it burns out. A flower gives its strongest scent when it matures and is about to lose its petals. So too will the dark powers, the forces of evil, escalate their deceptions in the world just before it's ended.

All of nature will be at God's service as he sends earthquakes, torrents of rain, hailstones, and sulfur. "The fish in the sea, the birds in the sky, the beasts of the field, every creature that moves along the ground, and all the people on the face of the earth will tremble at my presence. The mountains will be overturned, the cliffs will crumble and every wall will fall to the ground" (Ezek 38:20). God will call out to every bird and wild animal to come feast on the flesh of mighty men who had come against his land of Israel.

With all of this in the balance, the Spirit of God will strengthen us to where we, collectively from all cultures, are brought to stand on the other side of that barrier of water. The instruction was to know him, birthed into his Spirit. The message is unchanging, not bending to fit political correctness when first it sanctions oppressions of the government then changes as it preaches acceptance of every practice and belief in the world because now it's politically correct.

When treaties were signed there was an understanding that there would be future generations. When the ceremonies continued through all these years there was an intent to preserve the lands for the ones yet to be born. "Posterity will serve him; future generations will be told about the Lord. They will proclaim his righteousness, declaring to a people yet unborn" (Ps 22:30). It is a relationship made real only by the responsibility given to each. "How beautiful you are, my darling, how beautiful you are!" (Song 1:15). "How handsome you are, my beloved, and so pleasant!" (Song 1:16). The beloved Christ is presented in his beauty, his kindness, so that others are attracted and want to find him too. We are found in our wilderness, led safely to the marriage feast under his protections, his joy in us. Our focus is on him; we are lovesick when we can't find his presence. True teachings from God's Spirit regenerate this beloved relationship. New relationship is born from relationship with him. How different our history would be for us all had the true message of Jesus first been brought to the lands of North America.

European rulers sent not only true Christian missionaries to North America. They sent enforcers of a nominal state church to carry out the tactics that had been used by the Roman Empire. True believers were getting caught in the crossfire, persecuted, and executed back in Europe. Individuals living among the Indians who understood the Christ's view of their equality were pushed to the side. There they once stood, each dressed in their own clothing, with their different languages and separate heritages, sustained by the land, whether through words or through a gentle rainfall, each hearing God saying "I am here." Amid the travesties we now know as history, word of the newly discovered lands were brought back to Britain, and a Protestant coalition called the Aborigines' Protection Society lifted their voices against the treatment of Aboriginal peoples. Segregationist policies began to affect change among those wanting to change Indians into European workers. But that was not the majority story.

Following Europe's expansion to the shores of North America was the cultural dominance of a man, rather than many men serving the community. They demonized the victims to make it more acceptable. Disease wiped out whole communities, sometimes intentionally. The forced cultural changes came along with alcohol and drugs. Domestic violence took root.

Stories tell of a man meeting Peacemaker. The man was looking into a pot where he was boiling a human he had killed. Since Peacemaker was not getting an answer at the man's door, he climbed onto the roof and looked down the chimney. When the man saw Peacemaker's reflection in water in the pot, he thought it was himself. Seeing such a beautiful man in himself, his thoughts were transformed. He took the remains of the human outside to bury. He went to the stream to collect fresh water. Peacemaker went to find venison, and the two met back at the house to eat together.

As they ate, Peacemaker spoke about his vision of righteousness and justice, of orenda, the spiritual that is held by all beings. He talked of how these could lead the people into a Way of Peace. As the man listened, he felt a gentle wind stir his heart. A new vision began to rise in him.

Women today talking about solutions don't ask for stiffer punishments, jail sentences, or to cut men off from the community. Restoring a man relies on their tradition. In response, Akwesasne instituted programs to remind their men of the tradition of men and the value of women in their heritage. The relics of a feudal system are shown to them so they may become aware of where their wrong-mindedness originated. When a man is feeling this way, it's a loss. It's a form of grief. Condolences are needed. When he starts to heal himself, it's a form of recovery. When the man saw Peacemaker's face in a pot of water, he thought it was his own reflection. It was a very handsome face. He couldn't believe it was him. The third time he believed it was him and he thought about what he'd done in life.

Those actions didn't go with such a handsome face, so he lamented the ways he had followed. "I will never do that again," he said. He looked back up at the lodge and saw Peacemaker standing there. He walked up, wanting to share, so excited. "I changed my life," he told Peacemaker. "I used to practice this evil thing." Peacemaker congratulated him for his decision he made for self and earth. So, today, every man needing restoration has something he's hiding inside. When something is suppressed in a human, it builds up. In family abuse, that's what happens to men.

A man is emasculated when he is promiscuous, unfaithful, irresponsible, or violent in words or action. What is more masculine than a man who is trusted and able to keep the covenant of trust with his family, community, and God? Peacemaker reflected in self is an understood concept. There is a heritage to remind the people who they are in their communities.

Medieval law gave a man the right to smack his wife or give her a look to put her in her place if she spoke up. Follow that root up to 1492–1593 and see how that came to affect their sons. So when we try to reverse this, it takes a long time.

The Bible story of the formation of the universe uses the word for create, *bara*, to tell "In the beginning God created the heavens and the earth" and all of the living beings that dwell here. In that part of the world, in the Arabic language, the word's meaning includes to strengthen, make well, grow. All of these things were in the divine decree when the Giver of Life spoke the forces of nature into motion that would continue water flows through generations, renewing, strengthening, and growing.

The words of the Christ are now coming from the mouths of Natives who have sought to understand his teachings in the context of their own heritage. They present Jesus as a desirous image full of compassion and ability to care for others. Only Jesus can understand the world of a European, an Asian, a North American Native, a bear, a fish, and even a bird.

Circles have formed around the continent in worship of Christ. Flutes play, sage is burned, the sounds of rattles and drums come together to worship Jesus in the Native way. In 1998 Jim and Faith Chosa established Day Chief Ministries and the Red Earth Church in the Wilderness in Yellowtail, Montana. Jim, a member of the Keweenaw Chippewa Band in Michigan, is a member of the Apostolic Council for the International Coalition of Apostles. Faith is a member of the Apsaalooke (Crow) tribe. They work at bringing about relationship between Natives and non-Native cultures, all part of the body of Christ, and for the Apsaalooke Nation developing the Apostolic Asheta'ale Alliance.

Making use of Internet technology, they nurture the traditions of their people and emphasize their ability to defend their people. In the past the young would grow up being trained in warfare. They disciplined themselves in how to respond from the time of youth. They would map out the area's resources as well as the enemy's territory. They would do this so they could defend their families, their communities, their nations.

Today's call for warriors is to a spiritual battle. "For our struggle is not against flesh and blood, but against the rulers, against the authorities, against the powers of this dark world and against the spiritual forces of evil in the heavenly realms" (Eph 6:12).

6

One Bowl One Spoon

> If you follow my statutes and keep my commandments and observe them faithfully, I will give you your rains in their season, and the land shall yield its produce, and the trees of the field shall yield their fruit.
>
> LEVITICUS 26:3–4

THE TWO-ROW WAMPUM EXTENDED the guidance of the belt of the Dish with One Spoon. This is a short belt of white beadwork, with the circle of purple in the center symbolizing a field that is for everyone to hunt and gather. The principles embedded in the belt contain giving thanks and taking only what you need. This ancient acceptance is reflected in the Condolence Ceremony when a new roiane is raised into position. A feast is held with nothing sharp nearby as the bowl is passed to each roiane and each makes sure there is enough to go all the way around as he takes some for himself.

Peacemaker said, "Do not ever disagree, thus there shall always be unanimity! It will be like a single person; you will have one body, and one head, and one heart, which means that as we became one family, when we unified, creating relatedness and kindness, each person will now be kind to one and all. Moreover, we have completed all matters that follow the family through the generations, and these shall last as long as the earth exists, and as long as they are going to grow, the grasses and also the various weeds, and as long as the shrubs keep growing wild, the various shrubs, and as long as they keep growing wild, the trees, all kinds of trees, and as long as springs merge the water of rivers will keep flowing, also the large rivers and the various lakes; and as long as the sun keeps rising and setting and the moon keeps up its phases, and in the sky the stars do the same, and the wind is stirring on the land, and heavenly bodies continue to provide light by day and by night; thus, it shall last, the task we are completing, the Great Law, and these two will cooperate, the earthly land and the other one, the heavenly land."

At one time nearly two hundred neighboring nations accepted the One Bowl One Spoon. The people could travel as far as James Bay in the north, down to the coast of Florida, and out to the Atlantic and in every place count on being cared for and working together. When Europeans came, the Haudenosaunee wove the beads of the Two-Row Wampum to reconfirm how nations should live within the One Bowl One Spoon.

Humankind is the youngest member to enter the creation. God advised us to learn: "Ask the animals, and they will teach you, or the birds of the air, and they will tell you; or speak to the earth, and it will teach you, or let the fish of the sea inform you. Which of these does not know that the hand of the Lord has done this? In his hand is the life of every creature and the breath of all mankind" (Job 12:7–10).

Centuries later Christ's disciples continued the covenant into a new era. "For since the creation of the world God's invisible qualities—his eternal power and divine nature—have been clearly seen, being understood from what has been made, so that people are without excuse" (Rom 1:20).

Birds nest each in a tree, sharing all the sky and land as a resource intended for their food. The porcupine shows how to wear our defenses and yet remain softhearted, the squirrel how to store supplies for the coming winter. Scientists develop new technology by studying the insects. Plants tell us how there may be an impostor look-alike that causes sickness if we don't pass on knowledge of how to discern the true medicine. Flowering plants and fruit trees grow in their own specialized soils, each needing its own amount of light, all living as a community. A tree grows and brings thought of the tree of life, a reflection of all that is important to our God. "It is He who sits above the circle of the earth" (Isa 40:22), upholding all things.

"If you besiege a town for a long time, making war against it in order to take it, you must not destroy its trees by wielding an ax against them. Although you may take food from them, you must not cut them down. Are trees in the field human beings that they should come under siege from you?" (Deut 20:19).

Knowledge of herbs such as yarrow, meadowsweet, mugwort, chamomile, dandelion, cowslip, and raspberry were used by trained healers under the guidance of astrology. Each people group has a knowledge of the earth and sky and a way to live on the land.

The Hebrew people lived in reciprocal relationship with the land in awareness of what ancestors survived for them to be here. God, expressing the importance of homeland through the generations, tells his people, "You will live in the land that I gave to your forefathers; so you will be my people, and I will be your God" (Ezek 36:28).

The peoples of different languages, with different songs to sing and diverse knowledge of land, came together on the North American continent and had much to learn from each other. It brought realization that each of our cultures are only one part of God's plan. Our actions affect others.

"I brought you into a plentiful land to eat its fruits and its good things. But when you entered you defiled my land, and made my heritage an abomination" (Jer 2:7).

"It will be made a wasteland, parched and desolate before me; the whole land will be laid waste because there is no one who cares" (Jer 12:11).

"How long will the land lie parched and the grass in every field be withered? Because those who live in it are wicked, the animals and birds have perished" (Jer 12:4).

The instruction of Jeremiah in 6:16 would mean a specific thought to the Native people of the Americas. "Stand at the crossroads and look; ask for the ancient paths, ask where the good way is, and walk in it, and you will find rest for your souls."

Although the white man took away much of the land, the land is still there. Native nations worldwide seek costewardship of lands. The Onondaga Nation has been forming unique multicultural and multiracial partnerships throughout their original homeland to protect it. The efforts are hoped to result in economic revival that will benefit every community in central New York. The nation joined with the town of Tully to stop a gravel mine. They sent delegates with maps and photos of Superfund sites to conference rooms near Albany, where the delegates spent hours with an assortment of environmental advocacy groups ranging from the Natural Resource Defense Council to the American Lung Association. Residents reached out to the nation for help in fighting issues such as phosphorous in the water and a proposed Walmart. They worked with African American women on the south side of Syracuse to stop a sewage dump that utilized 1970s technology. The nation joined citizens in the fight against two proposed coal plants, one next to an elementary school that would bring in one hundred coal trains containing CO_2 that could not be sequestered. Residents asked their help in stopping a proposed pig farm in treaty lands near Montezuma National Wildlife Refuge, because the state had inadequate regulations. It's all about healing land, water, and our relationships.

The Haudenosaunee Environmental Task Force issued one of the first documents calling for a ban to protect water from hydrofracking. In August 2009 HETF visited Bradford, Pennsylvania in response to Aiello's hydrofracking to access the pockets of natural gas in the forested hills. Hydrofracking is a process of mixing some fifty-four chemicals into a slurry of water and sand, then digging as far as 1,100 feet below ground to pump the slurry into the earth to break the shale and release the gas. Most of the chemicals are known irritants to skin, eyes, and sensory organs, cause respiratory, gastrointestinal, and liver distress, and affect the brain, nervous system, and heart. Half affect kidneys and the immune system, cause developmental difficulties, and are known to affect ecology. A third are known carcinogens and mutagens and affect reproduction. Enforcement policies are few.

The 2005 Energy Policy Act sponsored by Vice President Dick Cheney exempted oil and gas from most environmental laws. Under the Bush administration hydrofracking was exempted from regulations of the Safe Drinking Water Act. The Onondaga Nation took the lead in preventing drilling deep into the Marcellus and Utica shales of their ancestral lands, protected by the treaties of Fort Stanwix of 1768 and of 1784, the Treaty of Fort Harmar of 1789, and the Treaty of Canandaigua of 1794. Their voice carries implications for other societies beyond their own. On Vancouver Island in Canada, the Hupacasath, a First Nation of about 280 members, filed a legal challenge against the government for not being consulted over implications the Foreign Investment Promotion and Protection Agreement (FIPPA) could have on its aboriginal rights and titles. The federal constitution obligates the government to consult with First Nations on matters that could affect them.

The government has been working to secure investment agreements with China at a time when the Chinese Communist Party is being questioned about squashing movements for human rights in the world's most populous country. If a crackdown on civil unrest follows, the Department of Foreign Affairs, Trade and Development Canada would have to uphold its guarantee toward rule of law and respect for human rights, causing an impact on international economics. China has interest in procuring Canadian resource-based companies. FIPPA could impact First Nation land claims and traditional territories. The lawsuit filed by the Hupacasath examines Canada's right to sign FIPPA without consulting First Nations. The case is supported by critics of FIPPA who say agreements with China could reverberate negatively through the country.

In the United States, although the Supreme Court has ruled that Indian title is "as sacred and as securely safeguarded as is fee simple absolute title," the Court has also ruled that "Indian title is primarily a permissive right to occupy certain land but the fee title remains with the United States government." Bringing this to an end requires a recognition of its roots in the 1823 *Johnson v. McIntosh* decision that brought the Doctrine of Discovery into US law. Thomas Johnson purchased land from the Piankeshaw Nation in the Midwest in 1773 and 1775. His descendants inherited the land. Then William McIntosh got hold of a federal land patent to the same land. The Johnsons brought action against McIntosh because they retained ownership given by the Indians. Chief Justice John Marshall held that Christian European nations assumed "ultimate dominion" over the lands of America and Indians had lost any rights to it. Marshall applied the religious edict to assert the "discovery gave title to the government, by whose subject, or by whose authority, the discovery was made, against all other European governments." To get around the US Constitution prohibiting religion playing a part in the country's laws, he cited the English charter issued to John Cabot authorizing him to take possession of lands. He affirmed that the country's law is based on the Law of Nations, emphasizing phrases like "European discovery of land" and dropping the word "Christian." This happened in the background of the same year James Madison wrote: "Religion is not in the purview of human government. Religion is essentially distinct from civil government, and exempt from its cognizance; a connection between them is injurious to both." Again in 1955 the Supreme Court held that Indian title is "a permissive right only" and that the title "is in the United States with the Indians having a temporary possessory right terminable at will by the United States without Constitutional liability."

The Tee-Hit-Ton, people of the Tlingit in Alaska, sought justice in the court for lumber taken from land they occupied, asking for a ruling that Indian title is a property right under the Fifth Amendment. The Supreme Court held that land occupied by Indians is not a property right but a right to occupancy "which the sovereign grants and protects against intrusion by third parties." It further stated that "Indian occupation of land without government recognition of ownership creates no rights against taking or extinction by the United States protected by the Fifth Amendment or any other principle of law." Again the Court circumvented the Constitution that provides all Native property is entitled to protection.

At a profound level the Doctrine of Discovery is not about Christianity. It's about a converting land into non-Native hands. This became the cornerstone of US Indian policy. It was used to remove the Cherokee on their Trail of Tears, to break treaties that are the "supreme law of the land" according to the Constitution, to steal homelands of thousands of people in the Indian Removal Act of 1835, to take ninety million acres of their land under the General Allotment Act of 1887, and to violate the 1868 Treaty of Fort Laramie to take the Black Hills away from the Lakota people—to name a few instances.

The prayers of the oppressed rise to God, a sovereign Creator who is merciful and requires justice. We are called to judge ourselves as a church, as a country, as a neighbor.

Disciples of Jesus asked how to pray and Jesus began with "Our father in heaven, hallowed be your name." His words echoed those in the garden of Eden when Adam and Eve were told they could have all good things the Lord had made but not to eat from the tree of knowledge. This was instruction not to make our own rationale be what rules our decisions to serve our own agendas, thinking we have so much knowledge we no longer need to consult the One who had created all. "Trust in the Lord with all your heart and lean not on your own understanding" (Prov 3:5). Choosing that tree of knowledge resulted in the downfall rippling through all creation.

When Mohawk elders noticed that black ash trees were disappearing, Les Benedict, assistant director of the St. Regis Mohawk Tribe's Environment Department, and Richard David, assistant environmental director for the Mohawk Council of Akwesasne, began gathering the tree's seeds to preserve the tree's future. Their efforts resulted in 60,000 saplings planted by Haudenosaunee communities. To insure their future, thousands of seeds have been placed in storage that will preserve them for a hundred years.

The black ash is used for its splints that bend into traditional baskets. It's also valued by the original people for its bark and leaves that treat fever and kidney infections. The tree provides seeds for red-winged blackbirds, grosbeaks, and other birds. To small mammals, deer, and moose, the tree is a food source, especially during the months of winter. Its branches give nesting sites and its root systems improve water quality for aquatic life. The ash was obscure until the invasive emerald ash borer threat spread to seven billion North American trees, fallen over in the forests, hollowed and dying alongside streets. The knowledge of Benedict and David was sought out and they began to travel far and wide hosting workshops on other reserves, at nature centers, and in universities, wherever they are invited to teach others about the ash's plight and the need for helping hands to gather the clusters of winged seeds in the fall. Under the guidance of the One Bowl One Spoon Wampum, a diverse group of people gathered at Nelson Swamp State Forest on the morning of May 2007 for the foundational Black Ash Center, established during a two-day conference at State University of New York College of Environmental Science and Forestry in Syracuse.

Present with Les and Richard were people from the Environmental Science and Forestry Ranger School, the Akwesasne Task Force on

Environment, the American Friends Service Committee, the Haudenosaunee Environmental Task Force, the Seneca Nation of Indians, South Nation Conservation in Canada, Maine Basketmakers, and the US Forest Service. The woodland, southeast of Syracuse, is a place of meadows, woods, and groves of cedar and pine infused with the strength of the sun. Once this area was logged for timber and owned by farmers. The tall trees and their young now share haven with four hundred species of vascular plants, including the endangered striped coral root and threatened spreading globeflower. More than a hundred species of birds fly into the arms of the trees. Chipmunks and squirrels forage. Night animals sleep. The value to the Lord is evident. "Are not five sparrows sold for two pennies? Yet not one of them is forgotten in God's sight" (Luke 12:6; Matt 10:29). Jesus as a man, a carpenter touching the tree bark, smoothing the grain, worked with a full understanding of the tree's function in creation and all who depend on it for shelter, food, cradles for the young, and coffins for the dead. Aware of its beginning and seeing its future struggle, he worked and built for the people's needs, realizing he would soon be nailed to a tree. Conceptions are shifting from development to what heals human and natural communities, using nature as a mentor to integrate relationship. In today's world the One Bowl One Spoon is a blueprint to understand that earth belongs to our God, designed to support everyone, and as they work they get to know each other, share knowledge, and promote a better understanding. It exhorts a lack of sharp words. They are not to sit down with a knife and be divisive. It's a method in which we act as one people.

This was the main message of the leaders who sat down as a league with Peacemaker. That's why waters and lands did not have boundaries between the six nations. This is a metaphor for the spiritual too. One Bowl One Spoon teaches much.

The prayer Jesus spoke, "Our Father, who is in heaven . . .", was about lifting our eyes and trusting Wisdom's precepts.

In Romans 9:3–5 Paul said, "For I could wish that I myself were cursed and cut off from Christ for the sake of my people, those of my own race, the people of Israel. Theirs is the adoption to sonship; theirs the divine glory, the covenants, the receiving of the law, the temple worship and the promises. Theirs are the patriarchs, and from them is traced the human ancestry of the Messiah, who is God over all, forever praised!"

Heritage remained meaningful.

Paul recounted how he confronted Peter in a dispute sometimes called the Incident at Antioch, over Peter's reluctance to share a meal with Gentile Christians. Writing of that time, Paul says, "I opposed him to his face, because he was clearly in the wrong." He told Peter, "You are a Jew, yet you live like a Gentile and not like a Jew. How is it, then, that you force Gentiles to follow Jewish customs?" (Gal 2:11–14). It would take time to work out these new relationships and eventualy agree that the message for everyone is "that a person is not justified by the works of the law, but by faith in Jesus Christ" (Gal 2:16).

Paul continued to attend temple, now holding out the fulfillment of what their old prophets had taught. At the same time he understood that Christ was asking us each to care about the other.

"For this reason I bow my knees before the Father, from whom every family in heaven and on earth derives its name, that He would grant you, according to the riches of His glory, to be strengthened with power through His Spirit in the inner man, so that Christ may dwell in your hearts through faith" (Eph 3:14–17).

"Our desire is not that others might be relieved while you are hard pressed, but that there might be equality. At the present time your plenty will supply what they need, so that in turn their plenty will supply what you need. The goal is equality" (2 Cor 8:13–14).

"In the throne room God spoke: 'I am making everything new'" (Rev 21:5).

Paul wrote in 1 Corinthians 12 of the many gifts the Holy Spirit gives to benefit the empowerment of others. That diversity promotes unique individuality among God's people that strengthens the group, reflective of the creation.

In 1 Corinthians 12:4-7 he reminded, "There are different kinds of gifts, but the same Spirit distributes them. There are different kinds of service, but the same Lord. There are different kinds of working, but in all of them and in everyone it is the same God at work. Now to each one the manifestation of the Spirit is given for the common good."

Christ not only created a church of people spanning across time and all its generations, across cultures and all the lands of desert, mountains, valleys, and forests, but he is the author of creation.

Paul says of Jesus, "He is the image of the invisible God, the firstborn over all creation. For by him all things were created that are in heaven and that are on earth, visible and invisible, whether thrones or dominions or principalities or powers. All things were created through him and for him" (Col 1:15-16). John, speaking of Jesus, says: "All things were made through him, and without him nothing was made that was made" (John 1:3).

Expressions of our thanksgiving—clapping hands, playing musical instruments, dancing, singing psalms and hymns, making a joyful noise, lifting our hands, being still, or shouting—recognize the gifts of creation, and, "on earth as it is in heaven," bring the joy of heaven down to earth.

Autumn fades the colors of summer, transforming meadows and tree lines into textures. The cold of midnight spreads further into the day. Earth tilts on her axis, rolling into winter to pull a blanket of snow over her, taking all the warmth into herself as she sleeps. The wind and sun play in the snow, blowing drifts off trees, sparkling in the sunlight as they fall through the air.

Our hope renews with spring's return.

In springtime snow recedes back into the earth. Fields fill with water to bring back the geese. Birds follow the northward rivers and fly to migrate. The people feel their feet on the earth again. They see the mercy in the blue sky. They see the water carry away the frozen ice. Reaching solstice, there's celebration of having survived the cold in order to welcome another birth of spring.

Writers of the Bible expressing the cycles of creation also used *bara* to encompass spiritual restoration. Psalm 51:10 says, "Create in me a clean heart O God, and renew within me a steadfast spirit." God's answer to this prayer restores thankfulness and good mind. Isaiah 57:18 says, "I will guide him and restore comfort to him, creating praise on the lips of the mourners in Israel. Peace, peace, to those far and near, says the Lord. And I will heal them."

The unsaved don't give thanks. They are not renewed to God.

The Law of Peace prepared the Mohawk for the onslaught that came upon them. It set the path out ahead of the people as onkwehonwe—"onkwe" meaning physical being and "honwe" meaning real, original things, a people who carry on knowledge of how to interact in our world. Health, coming from the word skenno, good message, invokes sun and rain on the land that makes way for babies to come, for trees to come, for all life to come. Spiritual vision sees restoration so we can perceive our abundance and not fear there won't be enough for everyone.

The Scriptures say, "He sends the springs into the valleys; They flow among the hills. They give drink to every beast of the field; the wild donkeys quench their thirst. By them the birds of the heavens have their home; they sing among the branches. He waters the hills from His upper chambers; the earth is satisfied with the fruit of Your works" (Ps 104:10–13).

Over time, we can forget. "Woe to those who add house to house and join field to field till no space is left and you live alone in the land. The LORD almighty has declared in my hearing: 'Surely the great houses will become desolate, the fine mansions left without occupants. A ten-acre vineyard will produce only a bath of wine, a homer of seed only an ephah of grain" (Isa 5:8-10).

Subdivisions focusing on only one property owner's perspective changes the entire landscape of animals. Deer cannot migrate to sustain their young. Predators like bobcats eating snowshoe hares clean out the area quickly. Black bears no longer have their terrain. Little animals like mole salamanders have lost their corridors. Prophecies talked about a new deer coming. Hunters now see half-white, half-brown speckled deer, turning white from malnutrition. It's a signal we are getting close to the world crumbling. As stewards appointed to oversee God's great gardens, what will we, the seventh generation of Europeans on this land, leave to the next seven generations for them to steward as a resource to the generations beyond them?

The Haudenosaunee looked to fields that their families before them had left for them and found that Haudenosaunee farmers contoured fields out of warm season grass to build organic content in the soil, holding off erosion and runoff and giving back a space to sandpipers, eastern meadowlarks, northern shrikes, bobolinks, harriers, as well as nesting areas for threatened and endangered species. They noted how the big and little bluestems, Indian grass, grama grass, and switch grass extend their root systems six feet below the ground to survive fires and storms. They made the decision to replant Native flora and fauna and promote the concept among non-Natives.

The Haudenosaunee utilize satellite systems circling the earth and transmitting aerial photographs to interpret and map lands, trails, and historic sites. They show if plants and animals still have a corridor or if the places ancestors moved through are now Superfund sites, dammed waterways, or heavily industrialized areas. Technology is letting them predict the effect of different decisions on the future.

When the roiane implement the One Bowl One Spoon, they are supporting the will of Creator in a way that was given to them. They stand as trees, connecting to the sky, rooted deeply in earth, nourished by the fountain of life. They consider if a decision will improve life for unborn generations and benefit ecology. They judge an action for its effect on peace, not just peace for people but for the natural world as well. After they answer these questions positively, they will step into a project.

In the 1990s carbon emissions fell to one percent, but since year 2000 the world's CO_2 emissions have almost tripled. The change has plants and animals marching northward. Sugar maples will move to Quebec. Insects and birds will follow. The boreal forest in northern New York will begin to see the Deep South's loblolly pine trees. The forests have already experienced a two degree Celsius warming. Warmer soil releases more carbon monoxide.

Preparing for change has merged groups from all over earth to understand what is coming. To heal the land means a return to working within higher law that governs nature. It's the "hallowed be your name" that leads to understanding there is a higher governance than our ever-changing policies.

The position of Commissioner of Indian Trade was established in the War Department in 1806 to herd the Native people into ways that would best serve the new country. In 1819 Congress passed the Civilization Fund Act, which lasted until 1873, to provide for the government and churches to work together to "civilize" Indians with the use of missionaries.

Among them, Rev. Eleazer Williams worked with the Ogden Land Company and the War Department, being paid well to remove the Indians to make way for the expanding Empire State. As church correspondence reveals, Eleazer had written about being invited to visit Washington during the winter of 1820 and had various interviews with the Secretary of War on the policy of removing the Eastern Indians to the West. In an 1833 letter from Eleazer to David Ogden, Eleazer wrote: "I have relied much upon the promises of the different trustees ever since 1819 for assistance in the 'great cause' in which I have been engaged and ultimately with a liberal and handsome compensation." Eleazer's tactic pitted Christian Indians against "pagan" Indians and within two decades all but about two hundred Oneida had left for Green Bay, Wisconsin, or the Thames River in Ontario. Missionaries were paid by both the Ogden Land Company and the US government to look for lands near Green Bay, Wisconsin. The Oneida sense of nationhood is expressed in a letter Eleazer wrote in 1833, saying, ". . . and the great exertion of the Chiefs to keep their people together, is worthy of all praise." The

Indians were seeking survival as a people. Few wanted to move. The first left in the fall of 1840 when about 244 traveled to Buffalo and boarded a boat.

The white paternalism of the past implies that the people's knowledge is not important to God, yet the greatest change Christianity has brought to North America has been in non-Natives facing the reflection of their own history.

In summer 1990 a simmering dispute erupted into a standoff between Kanesatake Mohawk and the town of Oka, Quebec. A messenger was sent to the councils of the League in the states, carrying a wampum to let them know they had trouble. As has been custom, the council sent someone, John Mohawk, to go up and report back. The town wanted to develop a golf course and residential development on pinelands used by the Mohawk, land where ancestors were buried near Kanesatake. The Mohawks' land claim had been rejected in 1986. The people blockaded the roads. Shots were fired back and forth. A provincial police officer was hit and died. The confrontation resulted in changes in federal claims policies, but the issues of the Mohawk were left unresolved. Some eight thousand Mohawk on the Kahnawake reserve near Montreal have filed a $1 billion grievance because of 25,000 acres granted by France three centuries ago for non-Natives to rent land. Five municipalities built upon the land and do not pay rent. They filed a claim in 1994.

Dr. Thomas McDonald, a Métis pastor at Kanesatake, related an incident that occurred soon after the Oka incident, when tensions were still running high. A summer Bible school was in place for the Mohawk children to approach Christ through their own unique culture, language, and crafts. A group of well-off churches in the states thrust itself onto the reserve, deciding to set up a summer Bible school during the same week of the already-established Mohawk Bible school.

The local pastor could not dissuade the wealthy outside churches from disrupting the Mohawk community. It took many conversations for the pastor to make them understand that just showing up could be very dangerous, especially in an already volatile time of distrust of the neighboring non-Natives. He tried to make them understand that many Mohawk elders distrust white people and don't want them teaching and influencing their children. He explained that he could not give them free access to the gym, which is for community functions.

McDonald spoke of their preconceived ideas of what an Indian reserve needed. They may indeed have been directed by the Holy Spirit toward the

Mohawk reserve, but it was God's intent that they should learn more about how to conduct themselves with other cultures.

Other incidents have resulted in positive relationship. One man who was an archer came to a reserve thinking all Indians know how to shoot bows and arrows. By the time he left, he had taught the children how to make arrows. Everyone benefited from this new relationship that brought about opportunities to talk.

It must be remembered that there have always been individuals who formed trusted relationships. When the disciples had to find a right way to go to the Gentiles, they chose Barnabas. Barnabas, who had encouraged Paul when he converted from being a distrusted persecutor, was a man with the insight to see that Jesus was global. Many centuries later, as the newcomers pushed westward, they wanted more land. President Andrew Jackson determined to remove the Cherokee in Georgia, North Carolina, Tennessee, and Alabama, despite the fact they had fought with him against the British in 1815. Five missionaries were arrested and criticized when they refused to take the oath of allegiance against the Cherokee. Two were from the American Board, one Moravian, and two Methodist. Relationship is a process, bumping up on snags and stones along the way, but taking us from our past into a new formation.

It was not that long ago that there was no border through Akwesasne. There were not jurisdictions causing families of the Mohawk difficulties in visiting each other across the water, bringing bushels of berries to trade with fishermen, and baskets from black ash trees for use in births, deaths, and ceremonies, and for marriages, to remind couples to help each other as the tasks of life get heavy, bending us with tiredness.

Here there's limestone and dolostone a million years old. The bedrock is forty feet deep. Eels, once 42 percent of the biomass of the fishery, are now rare. They can spend some thirty years in a watershed before the Sargasso Sea calls to them, thickening them into a blackish-bronze before they return to their place of birth. The eels here are exclusively female. It's unknown if the cause is environmental or if females have always come here to live. In 2006 the New York Power Authority and Ontario Power Generation installed eel ladders to help them journey up the river.

Fish are returning as the water cleanses. Akwesasne has partnered with the US Geological Survey to restore native fish, reintroduce Atlantic salmon that have disappeared from the St. Lawrence River in the past century, restore lake sturgeon habitat to the St. Regis River, and develop a threatened and endangered species assessment in the St. Lawrence River.

As water cleanses, the gifts of each individual become apparent.

Today a gathering of elected officials, residents, along with health, business, education, and recreation representatives and members of the St. Regis Mohawk Tribe gather as the twenty-one-member Alcoa Massena Community Advisory Panel to discuss remediation. Upriver where waters swirl around 1,864 islands, Canada designated the St. Lawrence Islands National Park, known as Thousand Islands. Two centuries ago the French and Indian War occurred here and many Mohawk lost their lives. Today people come and go to collect medicinal plants, camp out with the Freedom School, launch boats, or hike. Trails lead through a place where the Mohawk work with the park on turtle recovery and habitats for at-risk species. A landing where there are beautiful huge boulders is inspiring, with petroglyphs of the Thanksgiving Address. Elders come here to share knowledge. Building these partnerships rekindles memories of their territories. When the power dam was constructed, it blocked memory of everything west of the dam.

Decades ago in Akwesasne, priests, rabbis, and pastors traveled to meet with leaders at Akwesasne and talk about God, creation, and the destiny of the people of Earth. They created an ecotone like that at the woodsedge, a place of meeting. There are Native evangelists who have taken up the message of Christ. They understand the culture, community concerns, and history. They don't carry the aggressiveness or preconceived plans that so often remind of past trauma and broken promises. They don't need to become qualified through textbooks attempting to explain protocols and world view, because they are of the people.

The sacred is returning with its cultural reminders. Kahon:ios (Cohoes Falls), north on the Mohawk River, is where the Mohawk people tested Peacemaker by asking him to climb a tree.

They sawed off the branch he sat on and he fell into the waters. When Peacemaker emerged unhurt, the Mohawk accepted that he was sent by Creator. The return to the place where he met with them was a return of the memory of him. Peacemaker came and the old men saw hope. The young men lifted daughters in their arms and gathered their sons to listen. The mothers heard the words of safety. The grandmothers heard assurance of tomorrow's world. The old men heard the fulfillment of prophecy.

God cared. Missionaries did not bring God's care to a land unknown to God. God had always been here.

Passing through hands for a thousand years, the wampum of the Confederacy's founding told them "Our work is now completed. Now you have these words to live by and govern yourselves. These words constitute a new mind, which is the will of Teharonhiawako, the Holder of the Heavens. There shall be Righteousness when men desire justice, Health when men obey reason, Power when men accept the Great Law. These things shall be given form in the Longhouse where five nations shall live as one family. In Unity there is power; these are the people of the Hotinonshonni. Their voice shall be the voice of the Great Law. All men shall hear this and find peace."

The offer of friendship found under the branches gave the freedom to serve our relationship with God, each in our own way. This came from a way of life based on recognizing how each member of creation brings a unique gift. We are dependent on the diversity of all the gifts serving a higher purpose.

The time the Peacemaker went to the five nations to get them to come out of terrible war, he talked to them about the changing seasons, when to plant and when to harvest. In his message he told the people how to prepare for the things to come in the future. Now the Law applies to global warming that concerns all of us. It's about the changing economy and a prophecy that's coming down on us all. Now the inherent diplomacy of the governance leads to a way to talk of Jesus, the one name that brings the hope of salvation to all.

On February 4, 2011, the Canadian Nuclear Safety Commission (CNSC) issued a transport license to Bruce Power for plans to transport sixteen decommissioned nuclear generators—1,600 tons of radioactive waste—through the Great Lakes, down the St. Lawrence River, across the Atlantic Ocean, to Sweden for recycling.

The approval came after hearings in September 2010 that included opposition from environmental groups and politicians of more than a hundred towns along the route. Bruce Power maintained that threats from moving the first of sixteen hundred-ton steam generators from its plant on a peninsula in Lake Huron, Ontario were negligible. Each unit would cost about $1 million to transport to a facility operated by Sweden's Studsvik recycling plant near the Baltic Sea coast. A few years later, after recycling, ten percent would return across the ocean and up the river to Bruce Power.

The Mohawk were not informed of the impending shipment through their territory and not consulted. Emails from environmental groups circulating up the river reached their leaders. In 1999 a resolution had been passed in Akwesasne that prohibited nuclear material from passing through the territory.

The water again was the element bringing a unity of purpose. Working with groups of environmentalists, politicians, and citizens along both sides of the river, the people's voice was able to halt the shipment.

In March 2011 Bruce Power delayed plans to ship the generators until there was further discussion and meetings with First Nations and Métis. Hearings on the American side must also take place.

The St. Lawrence River holds the stories of tens of thousands of events along its shores and upon its currents. Each generation continues the stories. Today they reflect a return to the Two-Row Treaty that takes on more personal meanings. Earth—she will take care of us in the long term. We fall upon her, or we stand upon her, for sustenance, for comfort, for shelter, and for renewal. The story now is not about jurisdictional rights but about responsibilities that cause us to examine our relationship with God.

7

Dark and Light Creations

But even if he does not, we want you to know, O king, that we will not serve your gods or the image of gold you have set up.

DANIEL 3:18

"Then God spoke. 'Let there be light,' and there was light. And God saw the light, that it *was* good; and God divided the light from the darkness" (Gen 1:3-4). "This is the message we have heard from him and proclaim to you, that God is light, and in him is no darkness at all" (1 John 1:5).

After coming to earth, Sky Woman birthed a daughter who became the bride of the spirit of the west wind and she grew large with pregnancy. The daughter died giving birth to twin boys—one of light and the other of darkness. When her mother, Sky Woman, died, her head was flung into the sky. She's called Grandmother Moon, reflecting light into the dark night, tracking time, regulating the monthly cycles of all female life, and controlling the rise and fall of the tides. All this is part of her promise to help turtle, who had helped her when she fell to earth. When the twins grew up they went about creating things in the natural world together. They created rivers, flowers, and eventually human beings, who were to be caretakers. The good-natured twin came to be known as Shonkwaya'tiso (The One Who Made Our Bodies). This does not mean the one who created the universe but rather refers to the method by which the Great Mystery created elements in our natural world. The twin of light would make a berry bush. The twin of dark would place thorns on it or make ivy poisonous. The brother of dark altered all that the brother of light would make. Together the twins gave humans part of each of their minds so that out of our mouths comes both praise and curses. Only the brother of light could breathe life into them. Three breaths were breathed into the mouths of humans to bring them to life. When we die, our breath returns to the winds, our bodies to the earth, the water inside our beings returns to the cycles of water that replenish life, and the electrical energies within us return to the thunders. The soul returns to the sky world, the place where grandmother, the Sky Woman, originated. Some say that in winter the Pleiades star constellation shows where the great tree of life stands in the sky world. During the Midwinter Ceremony the smoke rising from the longhouse drifts up toward the Pleiades as the people give thanks. The twins competed but always tied in the bowl game, lacrosse, dice, and wrestling. So they agreed that one would rule the day with eldest brother sun and the other the night with Grandmother Moon.

The people understood this meant balance. Light had creativity. Light could make life and bring about creations from the throne room in heaven. Dark brother could structure but couldn't create. The light brother created a rose. The dark brother created its thorns. From the rose's point of view, every animal in the world wanted to trample it, smell it, or hold it. To the rose, the dark brother was needed because he gave it a defense.

In the world the people knew they needed both twins. The dark brother had too much structure and could bring too much oppression. The light brother had too much creativity and could lose sight of boundaries. So when talking with those with traditional knowledge, they're thinking, "What do we do to balance the North American continent, the site of the biggest genocide in the world?"

As the ones with the ability to heal an injured animal or strengthen an ill tree, human beings were given the responsibility to help all life. God granted us a will to choose as deep a relationship with him as we desire. "Be wise as a serpent and harmless as a dove," Jesus said (Matt 10:16). The snake represents our earthly nature, the dove the sky world of heaven. Jesus explained the need for our physical nature to live under the guidance of the spiritual. He reconciled earth and heaven and restored balance for humanity. In this life we would need to understand this. Angels can materialize. They are fellow beings of the creation. But demons must have a body to occupy or they cannot do anything. In all the power of earth to birth so many lives, there would be none without the sunlight and winds that carry clouds that bring rain from above. Fire and water wash over us from the sky. It's told that as the human race multiplied our Maker sent us to the four corners of the world, each with our own language, instructed to give thanks with our knowledge of the land that supports us. One day we would come back together to determine a way for God's renewal to continue.

One year in Akwesasne a non-Native graduate student interned with the Mohawk environmentalists. He decided to get a ribbon shirt and live like the Mohawk. An elder asked him about this and he said, "It gives me family." This was profound. They told him that his Celtic ancestry probably mirrored theirs a lot. Original Celtic language contains similar beautiful thoughts. The words for truth, trust, and tree, for instance, are entwined in the same base word *dorw*, the oak tree, the enduring symbol of their celestial tree of life. The people have traditions that follow the seasonal renewals, songs that rejoice in the elements that hold life together, clans that God appointed to strengthen a sense of belonging and responsibility. Their country too was invaded. The United Kingdom went there, drew a border across their island claiming it as their jurisdiction, and enforced their own ways, forbidding the Irish people from using their native Gaelic language or carrying on their heritage of songs and dance. Their Gaelic names were forbidden and anglicized just as the Mohawk's had been.

The student went to Europe and visited his ancestral lands. Now this red-haired friend wears the ribbon shirt to show respect for the Mohawk, not to be like them. Mother Earth is a powerful mother. It's through this perspective that many Native people view Americans and Canadians as being defensive when it comes to justice. Their identity is cut off looking back only to a time their people came here to colonize. Deep down there's no sense of legitimacy. Because all relationship brought together by God is reciprocal, they wonder what it is that these non-Natives were sent to learn. The greetings of compassion, traditions of friendship, and the sharing of land have all been offered. In return the news of Jesus became tied to losing family, home, and health.

Many survivors of the residential school and adoption systems regained this belonging as they returned to their traditions of condolence. It's a return to holding the hands of their grandfathers, grandmothers, mothers, fathers, brothers, and sisters, and prizing the land that sustained them. Often tobacco is burned and the smoke rises to the Creator's world, carrying thanks. "Let my prayer be set before you as incense, the lifting of my hands as the evening sacrifice" (Ps 141:2). The wounds are deep.

Punishments and policies forbidding traditional prayer filled thousands of graves before it was stopped by the American Indian Religious Freedom Act in 1978. The act protects traditional religious rights, possession of sacred objects, and access to sacred sites, although it does not yet include protection of places of sacred meaning. Aboriginal rights in Canada have been protected since 1982.

A cultural shift has moved Western society from the structured rules of a monobelief into political correctness. "Your drums and pow wows are legal now," they say.

Society now studies the ancient wisdoms to apply to sociology, the study of the environment, and science. But research cannot discover everything. Research cannot entirely capture the movement of the Holy Spirit, creativity and joy moving like wind, or the way the Lord brings a new understanding of himself out of heartbreak. Often the deepest friendships are forged as people step forward through the wreckage in the humility of regrets. Understanding the curse that fell on humankind, that none of our efforts will make a perfect solution in this world, is fundamental to realizing we each are struggling under the same forces tearing at us. Sharing our stories brings knowledge of each other that creates bonds of shared experience and brand-new insights into the God of our salvation. The issue of what practices spiritually belong in the teachings of Christ is often ambiguous and left to each individual to choose for themselves as the Holy Spirit informs. Many peoples pray in trust toward the four directions that bring the cycle of returning seasons, and like the Haudenosaunee give thanks for the winds that pollinate the corn and bring them their future.

The Haudenosaunee speak of four Sky Dwellers who Creator assigned as messengers when creation was formed. They are called the four brothers—the east, north, west, and south. These four beings were sent with the arrival of Peacemaker, when ceremonies were given, when the clans were named. They are noticed when they come breezing through trees, watched carefully for their correlations to events. Leaders talk together about winds accelerating and how people treat their children with neglect and abuse. Both of these phenomena show the degrading of the earth. In 2000, 1.8 million children were forced into prostitution and pornography. More than one million were victims of trafficking, according to the United Nations Secretary-General's Study on Violence Against Children. Nearly 53,000 of the world's children were murdered in 2002. In 2004, 218 million children across the globe worked in child labor, more than half in hazardous jobs.

Entering land where people prayed toward earth's four directions, the Bible in the hands of newcomers held similar teachings. "He makes winds his messengers" (Ps 104:3).

When the Bible says "he brings out the wind from his storehouses" it talks about four winds. Cycles continuing growth, healing, and life require wind from the east where the sun rises, the wind from the north's cold lands, the wind from the west-setting sun, and the warm wind from the south. The spirit of the Lord instructed Ezekiel to bring life to the valley of bones by calling to the four directions. In Ezekiel 37:9 the prophet was instructed to pray, "From the four winds come in, O winds, and breathe upon these slain people that they may come to life." The winds came singing over the bones, standing them up and forming them back together.

Scripture acknowledges the east wind: "By warfare and exile you contend with her—with his fierce blast he drives her out, as on a day the east wind blows" (Isa 46:11). "From the east I summon a bird of prey" (Jer 18: 17). "Like the wind from the east, I will scatter them before their enemies" (Ezek 17:10). "An east wind from the Lord will come, blowing in from the desert; his spring will fail and his well dry up. His storehouses will be plundered of all its treasures" (Hos 13:15).

It was the east wind that parted the Red Sea. "And Moses stretched out his hand over the sea; and the Lord caused the sea to go back by a strong east wind all that night, and made the sea dry land, and the waters were divided" (Exod 14:21). In Exodus 10:13 we read, "And when it was morning the east wind brought the locusts." The west wind brought the deliverance. "And the Lord turned a mighty strong west wind, which took away the locusts, and cast them into the Red sea; there remained not one locust in all the coasts of Egypt" (Exod 10:19).

We are in relationship with the trade winds, the easterlies and westerlies, zephyr, chinook, foehn, sky sweeper, mistral, williwaw and Boreas, Santa Ana and pyrn, and all the others. They were here from creation's foundation, here when Jesus was born, as he rose to heaven they were doing their job. They will be here long after you and I finish. Solomon, who asked God for wisdom, learned to understand the laws that guide nature, the medicinal plants given for our health, the consequences of choices. People sought his knowledge. He writes in the Song of Solomon (4:16) about the need to bring winds. "Awake, north wind, and come, south wind! Blow on my garden, that its fragrance may spread everywhere." The south wind is mentioned in Psalm 78:26–27: "He caused the east wind to blow in the heavens and by His power he brought in the south wind. He also rained meat on them like the dust, feathered fowl like the sand of the seas." And consider Job 37:17: "You who swelter in your clothes when the land lies hushed under the south wind."

The currents of air warm and rise, drawing in from all around, sometimes two currents meeting to create a spiral motion like the one correlating to prophecy in Ezekiel 1:4, "Then I looked and behold a whirlwind was coming out of the north. A great cloud with raging fire engulfing itself. And brightness was all around it and radiating out of its midst like the color of ember out of the midst of fire."

The winds stand as servants attending God, a thought inspired by Psalm 104:4, about angels who pass between the place of earth and the place of heaven: "These chariots go forth to the four winds of heaven, after presenting themselves before the Lord of all the earth." If the wind blows rain clouds to us, carries chemical messages from tree to tree, swoops leaves into the river, or helps the birds to fly across hundreds of miles, it is following its instructions as a worker of creation. To pray toward all four directions holds meaning for the need for balance and recognition of the design of God. The writers of these verses understood, just as the Haudenosaunee practice, that we live centered in the varied gifts from the four directions.

"The wind blows wherever it pleases. You hear its sound, but you cannot tell where it comes from or where it is going. So it is with everyone born of the Spirit" (John 3:8). The Greek word the writer here used for wind is the same as for spirit. Jesus knew winds as beings with whom he could communicate. In Luke 8:22–25, when he and his disciples were in a boat the Sea of Galilee, Jesus fell asleep. The wind came up, blowing up fierce waves, rushing over the boat and buffeting the disciples. Frightened, they woke Jesus. He stood and told the wind to calm. The wind quieted and the sea steadied. The disciples wondered what manner of man could command the winds and sea. Jesus told them they should have more faith. He had said that only God's spirit could open their eyes to see the truths around them.

"Not by might or by power but by my spirit" (Zech 4:6).

The essence of the message is that we each can be restored but we cannot do it ourselves.

> The people living in darkness have seen a great light; on those living in the land of the shadow of death a light has dawned. (Matt 4:16)

> A light to lighten the Gentiles, and the glory of your people Israel. (Luke 2: 32)

> For this is what the Lord has commanded us: "I have made you a light for the Gentiles, that you may bring salvation to the ends of the earth." (Acts 13:47)

> It is too small a thing for you to be my servant to restore the tribes of Jacob and bring back those of Israel I have kept. I will also make you a light for the Gentiles, that you may bring my salvation to the ends of the earth. (Isa 49:6)

Christ warns:

> Not everyone who says to me, "Lord, Lord," will enter the kingdom of heaven, but the one who does the will of my Father who is in heaven. On that day many will say to me, "Lord, Lord, did we not prophesy in your name, and cast out demons in your name, and do many mighty works in your name?" And then will I declare to them, "I never knew you; depart from me, you workers of lawlessness." Then the King will say to those on his right, "Come, you who are blessed by my Father; take your inheritance, the kingdom prepared for you since the creation of the world. For I was hungry and you gave me something to eat, I was thirsty and you gave me something to drink, I was a stranger and you invited me in, I needed clothes and you clothed me, I was sick and you looked after me, I was in prison and you came to visit me." Then the righteous will answer him, "Lord, when did we see you hungry and feed you, or thirsty and give you something to drink? When did we see you a stranger and invite you in, or needing clothes and clothe you? When did we see you sick or in prison and go to visit you?" The King will reply, "I tell you the truth, whatever you did for one of the least of these brothers of mine, you did for me."

> Then he will say to those on his left, "Depart from me, you who are cursed, into the eternal fire prepared for the devil and his angels. For I was hungry and you gave me nothing to eat, I was thirsty and you gave me nothing to drink, I was a stranger and you did not invite me in, I needed clothes and you did not clothe me, I was sick

and in prison and you did not look after me." They also will answer, "'Lord, when did we see you hungry or thirsty or a stranger or needing clothes or sick or in prison, and did not help you?" He will reply, "I tell you the truth, whatever you did not do for one of the least of these, you did not do for me." (Matt 7:21–23, 34–45)

"Only, as the Lord has assigned to each one, as God has called each, in this manner let him walk. And thus I direct in all the churches" (1 Cor 7:17). "Let every man abide in the same calling wherein he was called" (1 Cor 7:20). "For in Christ Jesus neither circumcision nor uncircumcision has any value. The only thing that counts is faith expressing itself through love" (Gal 5:6).

Old Testament stories tell of a time the Israelites were taken captive by King Nebuchadnezzar, a ruler of the Babylonian Empire. His name in Hebrew, Nebu, means Protects the Crown. The soldiers took over Jerusalem and stole the sacred items from the temple to display in the king's house. The people no longer lived under their own governance. It had been prophesied in Isaiah 39:7: "And they shall take away some of your sons who will descend from you, whom you will beget; and they shall be eunuchs in the palace of the king of Babylon." This was six hundred years before Christ walked the earth as a man. Nebuchadnezzar took the best of Israel's future, the brightest young. Among the sons were Daniel, Hannaniah, Mishael, and Azariah. Their names were taken away and Daniel (meaning God Is My Judge) was renamed Belteshazzar (Bel's Prince); Hannaniah (Beloved by the Lord) was renamed Shadrach (Illumined by Sun-god); Mishael (Who Is as God) was renamed Meshach (Who Is like Venus); and Azariah (the Lord Is My Help) was renamed Abednego (Servant of Nego). They were indoctrinated into a new identity. For three years they were presented with the king's foods, and made dependent on Nebuchadnezzar as they were assimilated into service to his authority. But the young men could not be shaken from their heritage. They rejected the king's menu. With reason and diplomacy Daniel said, "Please test your servants for ten days, and let them give us vegetables to eat and water to drink. Then let our appearance be examined before you, and the appearance of the young men who eat the portion of the king's delicacies; and as you see fit, so deal with your servants." (Dan 1:12–13)

To spiritually survive in this world, they resolved not to take on the customs of a foreign country and not to eat their unhealthy foods. Steadfast in their identity and the faith they served, they learned the new knowledge that would be useful but never let it replace their own. Central to this was reverence for the way their elders had taught them to pray. When Daniel learned that a decree had been passed to enforce bowing down to foreign gods, Daniel went home "to his upstairs room where the windows opened toward Jerusalem. Three times a day he got down on his knees and prayed, giving thanks to his God, just as he had done before" (Dan 6:10). His people had been taught that "if they turn back to you with all their heart and soul in the land of their enemies who took them captive, and pray to you toward the land you gave their ancestors, toward the city you have chosen and the temple I have built for your Name; then from heaven, your dwelling place, hear their prayer and their plea, and uphold their cause" (1 Kgs 8:48–49). This Daniel did so under threats of death. The prophecies helped prepare him. He studied the Old Testament prophets, who had warned that while this would come upon them, God would end it. He knew the time of their release from Babylon was nearing.

In time the king would benefit from the knowledge of these young men. God's hidden plan manifested itself in the way Daniel and his friends responded to the Babylonians and were lifted up to be the country's administrators. God enabled Daniel to interpret dreams and withstand an attack by lions and a fiery furnace. As a result Babylon learned about the Hebrew beliefs and benefited from knowledge of their relationship with the living God, because these young men were willing to give up their lives rather than serve alien gods.

The February 8, 1899 edition of the *Syracuse Herald* reported that "Iroquois Were a miserable Lot of Devilish Savages." The report added, "It is necessary to have entire Control over them before Lasting Good will follow." A 1910 cartoon illustrated a field of Indians captioned with "The Weeds are Tall and the Scythe is small."

This was the Christian nation known to the original people. Similar stories ran across the country. In 1800s Colorado, Col. Chevington's battle against the Cheyenne celebrated how they cut out women's private parts and had them exhibited on a stick, and "not a body of a man, woman or child but was scalped." The form of churchianity that shed innocent blood across the world for two thousand years has bludgeoned the Anabaptists, Jews, Africans, and Australian Aboriginals, to name a few. Ignoring this past is like asking people to forget the deaths of their mothers and fathers.

The Creator of all things did not change his mind about the creation covenant, as evidenced when the psalmist invites "all you families of nations" (Ps 96:7) to ascribe to the Lord's glory and strength, and "Let the heavens rejoice, let the earth be glad; let the sea resound, and all that is in it. Let the fields be jubilant, and everything in them; let all the trees of the forest sing for joy. Let all creation rejoice before the Lord, for he comes, he comes to judge the earth" (Ps 96:11–13).

As truth comes to light it can capture minds in the accusations, drawing them into the territory of darkness, the prince of which is called the accuser. Paul admonishes us to understand that restoration to God is personal. He said, "One person considers one day more sacred than another; another considers every day alike. Each of them should be fully convinced in their own mind. Whoever regards one day as special does so to the Lord. Whoever eats meat does so to the Lord, for they give thanks to God; and whoever abstains does so to the Lord and gives thanks to God" (Rom 14:5–6). "Therefore let us stop passing judgment on one another" (Rom 14:13).

Accusation out of the days of our past are overcome by choosing to accept the prayer of Jesus: "I do not pray for these alone, but also for those who will believe in Me through their word; that they all may be one, as You, Father, are in Me, and I in You; that they also may be one in Us, that the world may believe that You sent Me. And the glory which You gave Me I have given them, that they may be one just as We are one: I in them, and You in Me; that they may be made perfect in one, and that the world may know that You have sent Me, and have loved them as You have loved Me" (John 17:20–23).

We who hear his call are in the wedding procession toward the celebration, men and women, old and young, under his protections as we walk, fragrant with his love, beaten up by the enemy, worn out and dirty, leaning on each other for support. But to his eyes, watching us persevere, we are beautiful, "awesome like an army with banners" (Song 6:4). Songs rise from among those in the procession moving toward Jesus, music lifting the others with its praise in every language, instrument, and dance of joy in the Lord's strength. Along this journey the churches began hearing the stories of the children and the communities who suffered from their removal. They began to look at their own history of suppression, the cases of abuse in residential schools, and the oppression of the truth. The people began coming together to talk about this.

On June 1, 2008 the Canadian government formed the Truth and Reconciliation Commission as part of the settlement agreement that had been negotiated between legal counsel for former students and legal counsel for the churches, government, Assembly of First Nations, and other Aboriginal organizations. The government had received some 99,460 applications for the Common Experience Payment.

Elders recommended the Commission begin with a ceremony that would bring spirituality into the issue, carrying healing through time. Go slowly, they said, and recognize where communities are in the process of getting ready to reconcile.

The Commission's 2012 report offered four guiding principles for a new relationship: mutual recognition, mutual respect, sharing, and mutual responsibility. Peacemaker once came across Lake Ontario rowing on clear waters full of healthy life. At each place he stopped there was a confluence with the people, an age-old message that carried, reminding people that "Love and faithfulness meet together; righteousness and peace kiss each other, faithfulness springs forth from the earth, and righteousness looks down from heaven. The Lord will indeed give what is good; and our land will yield its harvest" (Ps 85:10–12). Some seven million acres of Native lands that remained federally recognized by Canada and the US are still joined to each other by waterway's life-sustaining strength, a spiritual and physical strength that has become damaged.

Rivers and lakes flowing over and through earth melt into the Great Lakes' fragile ecosystem, covering 200,000 square miles. The lakes receive all this and send it on the St. Lawrence River's 1,200-mile journey to the edge of continent, where it forms a horizon between land and sky. Water reflecting sky above, reflecting to heaven our actions here on earth, returns to us as rain.

Water is our fluid connection to the land, an intended reciprocal relationship that has become damaged. In the US basin alone, there are more than fifteen hundred advisories against eating fish. Children are prevented from reaching their hands to touch its liquid grace. After the first ships entered the seaway in the spring of 1959 the Mohawk could no longer depend on the river's currents and the fish sustaining them. Many of the Mohawk men had to seek wages as ironworkers, living away from their families.

The missionary's authority, the books of the Bible, wanted them to remember, "He makes springs pour water into the ravines; it flows between the mountains. They give water to all the beasts of the field; the wild donkeys quench their thirst. The birds of the air nest by the waters; they sing among the branches. He waters the mountains from his upper chambers; the earth is satisfied by the fruit of his work" (Ps 104:10–13). The water from God is for everyone. But mixed together, tangled the way plants will grow together, the message was entwined with the developers and a money system that muted the thanksgivings and brought rape, racism, and greed in the fear that God wouldn't provide enough for everyone.

When the consequences began bearing down on us, environmentalists understood what the Mohawk had been warning since the 1800s. It would be water that in time brought the people together to recognize what now affects us all. The health of the river teaches us how our shared knowledge can benefit everyone.

Today the Mohawk work together with environmental agencies and local groups, schools and universities, on both sides of the river, focusing on restoring health. In Akwesasne partnership is spoken of as a respect encompassing social, political, and cultural views as well as communication in ways that allow for questioning. Equity in Western terms usually means money. It can include the provision to hire community researchers or an administrator. Equity can also be knowledge or a network of social and political power. It has to be transparent.

Empowerment is authorship. It can include training community people who will keep the skills in the community. It can include a way of translating information into strategies for the community. It means we accept our responsibilities.

Do these things and partners gain more respect for each other and find more equity, which brings more empowerment. The circle of peace is complete as we come closer together in a reciprocal relationship.

The Holy See supported the UN Declaration on the Rights of Indigenous Peoples, adopted on September 13, 2007, and with it recognized the fundamental human rights of indigenous peoples. Representatives affirmed the church's commitment to truth, peace, and reconciliation in its Periodic Report to the UN Committee on the Elimination of Racial Discrimination in 2000. The Holy See stated to CERD that local Catholic churches are tasked with the "defense of the rights of individuals and groups [and] denouncement of the injustices which are at the root of the evil."

Pope John Paul II's March 12, 2000 Universal Prayer affirmed "justice and truth must go hand-in-hand," and "Christians have been guilty of attitudes of rejection and exclusion, consenting to acts of discrimination on the basis of racial and ethnic differences." He added, "Let us pray that . . . Christians will be able to repent of the words and attitudes caused by pride, by hatred, by the desire to dominate others. . . . Let us pray for all those who have suffered offences against their human dignity and whose rights have been trampled."

Meanwhile, the Supreme Court has not rejected the Doctrine of Discovery but has upheld its extreme interpretation. Unless governments act on their constitutional responsibility, no taxation without representation, for instance, or preventing land claims that take an average of twenty-five years to resolve and extinguish ancestral rights, society will not be well.

The first footnote in the 2005 *City of Sherrill v. Oneida Indian Nation of New York* case comments on the doctrine, affirming that European Christians have more right to the land than people who have lived there since time immemorial: "fee title to the lands occupied by Indians when the colonists arrived became vested in the sovereign—first the discovering European nation and later the original States and the United States." The decision reverberated in April 2005 when, citing the *Sherrill* case, the governor withdrew legislation to settle claims.

In 1981 Federal Judge Neil McCurn said, "There is no question but that these cases present claims which long ago should have been solved in a legislative forum rather than a court of law. Unfortunately, neither the state of New York nor the federal government has shown much indication to do so thus far."

Twenty years later, in 2000, a jury determined the state had illegally stolen the 64,015 acres on the north side of Cayuga Lake from the Cayuga Nation in 1795 and 1807, and awarded the nation $37 million.

McCurn increased the settlement, ruling that the state pay land-claim damages totaling $247.9 million. In 2004, Gov. George Pataki issued a "Memorandum of Understanding" with the Cayuga Nation to give the $247.9 million over fourteen years and allow the people to establish up to ten thousand acres of sovereign land.

Then the US Second Circuit Court of Appeals cited the *Sherrill* decision and reversed Judge McCurn's decision. The Cayuga were left with nothing. The Cayuga did everything they could and New York State violated laws in acquiring their land, and yet the Second Circuit Court ignored it, brushed it aside.

Inspired by the Episcopal Church, other churches have been taking a stand on the Doctrine. Quakers in Toronto issued a formal statement at the Canadian Yearly Meeting on August 22, 2013.

> Friends are encouraged to explore further how we personally and corporately respond to how "discovery" is ingrained in our culture

and way of life. Canadian Yearly Meeting supports the process of building right relationship among peoples in Canada and we ask ourselves what the process of bringing reconciliation and healing means to us and to how we proceed.

The resolution repudiated the Doctrine of Discovery and encouraged the Canadian government to "examine how Canadian history, laws, practices and policies have relied on the Doctrine of Discovery and formally repudiate it, [and] reinterpret law to be consistent with the UN Declaration of the Rights of Indigenous Peoples and other international human rights standards."

In September 2009 a Quaker group in Philadelphia voiced support for the United Nation Declaration on the Rights of Indigenous Peoples. The Society of Friends renounced the Doctrine of Discovery, stating it is inconsistent with the teachings of Jesus. Conversations about the doctrine networked around the world. In 2010 former Penobscot Indian nation chief Jim Sappler called on national indigenous organizations to repudiate the doctrine and the laws and policies based on it. A resolution was drafted for the United South and Eastern Tribes and the National Congress of American Indians supporting approval of the Episcopal Church's call for justice.

All that's being asked is for the non-Natives to realize the doctrine's influence on history and how the Supreme Court uses it to override the Constitution when dealing with Indian people. Non-Natives are called to work toward changing their society to one of justice.

The Haudenosaunee are one of more than sixteen thousand people groups in the world. Of these, ten thousand are classified as being reached by missionaries in the last two thousand years. What knowledge are these indigenous peoples preserving that would enhance our collective understanding of our covenant with God, and enable us to implement decisions to help the next generation?

Ezekiel 31:4 tells of a tree. "The waters nourished it, deep springs made it grow tall; their streams flowed all around its base and sent their channels to all the trees of the field." Then the tree's death is noted in verse 15: "on the day it was brought down to the grave I covered the deep springs, and its abundant waters were restrained." Ezekiel 47:8–9 describes a vision of a river. Land is parcelled to the tribes of Israel, with the temple in the middle and the river running from the center that connected them all to each other. "When it empties into the sea, the water there becomes fresh. Swarms of living creatures will live wherever the river flows. There will be large numbers of fish, because this water flows there and makes the salt water fresh; so where the river flows everything will live." When that consciousness fell away, Hosea 4:2 prophesied: "There is no faithfulness, no love, no acknowledgement of God in the land. There is only cursing, lying and murder, stealing and adultery; they break all bounds, and bloodshed follows bloodshed. Because of this the land mourns, and all who live in it waste away; the beasts of the field and the birds of the air and the fish of the sea are dying." The passage continues, "So I will destroy your mother—my people are destroyed from lack of knowledge" (Hos 4:5–6).

The circle of the north spills through gateways entering the ocean, tossing up its waves, breathing with perplexity of the roaring changes pressing upon it. Where the St. Lawrence pours out all it has carried, it meets the cold current from the north, the Labrador Current that flows from the Arctic Ocean, as well as the warm Gulf Stream coming from the south. The two currents combine, together affecting climates in many places. "All streams flow into the sea, yet the sea is never full. To the place the streams come from, there they return again" (Eccl 1:7). A dire symphony of melting glaciers, spreading disease, severe weather, disappearance of a million species, change of ocean circulation, human water shortages, and routes of pollution affect the tasks of the currents. Warmer waters release contaminants in sediments to reenter water and air. Lowered oxygen shifts the biodiversity. Northern shrimp who thrive in low oxygen have survived. But cod are no longer here. And all the songs of thanks, with the tears of loss, intermingle in it. Winter comes early to Haudenoaunee homeland. Mother Earth needs to rest from birthing all her children. She is tired. The winds from the east and the north bring in a cold snow to cover her and let her sleep. The people are warm inside around the fire, listening to elders tell them the stories of their history, lessons, and creations. The grouse seek rest beneath a small conifer and fluff out their feathers for warmth. They may ground roost under snowfall, especially at night. God provided a plan.

The Mohawk prophecy speaks of a "long winter" coming. "Have you entered the storehouses of the snow or seen the storehouses of the hail, which I reserve for times of trouble, for days of war and battle?" (Job 38:22–23). The landscape becomes desolate, offering no provision. Hosea 6:3: "Let us acknowledge the Lord; let us press on to acknowledge him. As surely as the sun rises, he will appear: he will come to us like the winter rains, like the spring rains that water the earth."

"He has shown you, O mortal, what is good. And what does the Lord require of you? To act justly and to love mercy and to walk humbly with your God" (Mic 6:8). The earth spins, carrying us around the sun and through the Milky Way to a place in time that prophecy foretells. Fresh snowfall erases the world for a new landscape of new life to color when the south and west winds return again. The winds from the north come in their strength, carrying to those yet to be born all that we've left behind, whether the continued provision of earth's offerings and the knowledge of how to live together, whether thanksgiving or harshness, leaving only a memory of springtime buds pushing from the shelter of a rock. There's not a leaf on the trees. Not a blossom on the wildflowers. Even the squirrels have tunneled into shelters. Only the evergreens stand with their continuous green. The Great Mystery, the Giver of Life, inspired mention in Hosea 14:8: "I am like a flourishing juniper; your fruitfulness comes from me." At the top of the Tree of Peace sits an eagle whose exquisite vision sees negative forces that may bring harm. He spreads his wings over the people and he cries out in warning. He is called the guardian of the peace. Prophecy brought to the Haudenosaunee tells that earth will groan in birth pains from west to east, reminding that before a birth there is water, a great flood of waters, followed by labor contractions, spasms before new life. Earthquakes have been dreamt about that will shake the fault lines under the St. Lawrence River, widen the Niagara River, and damage the cities of Buffalo, Rochester, and Syracuse. The Moses-Saunders Dam, just west of Akwesasne, will break and the river's waters will run, finding their natural courses again. The ocean will rise and surge inland along the east coast. The Mississippi River will swell open to a fifty-mile gap slicing the country. The winds will be sent to carry volcanic ash around the world, blocking the sun. The polar axis will shift and warm. Tsunamis will overwhelm Europe, Indonesia, California, Peru, West Africa, Japan, and Texas. The North and South Americas will break apart.

Since the beginning of time the Creator has spoken to us in words of kindness and words of warning. "But they deliberately forget that long ago by God's word the heavens existed and the earth was formed out of water and by water. By these waters also the world of that time was deluged and destroyed. By the same word the present heavens and earth are reserved for fire, being kept for the day of judgment and destruction of ungodly men," Peter says in 2 Peter 3:5–7. In Isaiah 24:4–6 the Bible foresees, "The earth dries up and withers, the world languishes and withers, the exalted of the earth languish. The earth is defiled by its people; they have disobeyed the laws, violated the statutes and broken the everlasting covenant. Therefore a curse consumes the earth; its people must bear their guilt. Therefore earth's inhabitants are burned up, and very few are left."

Without its water, earth dries into a spinning ball of fire. Deep inside the earth temperatures rise about one degree Fahrenheit every sixty feet down. Earth's core is thought to be melting rock burning at an estimated 100,000 degrees, a center of heat from the time of earth's birth. A place of no water. Drink of the living waters, Jesus said. As pressures mount, with threats bearing down on a more globally conscious world, the battle between the dark and the light brings ever more to a renewal of covenant. They seek a promise like that between brothers in covenant prayer, that we would be one with each other, perfected in unity (John 17:21–23). We are called to be members of one body as members of one creation.

Christians now feel marginalized, viewing the world system as a negative they want to protect their children from so their beliefs and customs can continue to uphold faith in God. They look around for allies to stand with them in their values. They should remember that those allies will come from many nations and many peoples. The prophet Zechariah foresaw, "Many nations will be joined with the Lord in that day and will become my people. I will live among you and you will know that the Lord Almighty has sent me to you" (Zech 2:11).

When the Hebrew people were sent to possess a land it meant they would occupy it with prayer, worship, and God's ways of living in relationship to the land and each other. Extending this into the new covenant of Christ, we are to occupy with his Spirit, sustaining a heritage for our children to grow in and carry on.

Jesus told a parable about the balance between dark and light:

> The kingdom of heaven is like a man who sowed good seed in his field. But while everyone was sleeping, his enemy came and sowed weeds among the wheat, and went away. When the wheat sprouted and formed heads, then the weeds also appeared. The owner's servants came to him and said, "Sir, didn't you sow good seed in your field? Where then did the weeds come from?" "An enemy did this," he replied. The servants asked him, "Do you want us to go and pull them up?" "No," he answered, "because while you are pulling the weeds, you may root up the wheat with them. Let both grow together until the harvest. At that time I will tell the harvesters:

MENDING THE BROKEN LAND

> First collect the weeds and tie them in bundles to be burned; then gather the wheat and bring it into my barn." (Matt 13:14–29)

We are told to know that God is the same yesterday, today, and tomorrow. He is unchanging. From the first creation, *bara'*, the root word that means to separate or divide, the nature of that creation continues as we are sent to the time the dark and light forces will be separated again as they were for creation to be formed into day and night. "Let both grow together until the harvest" (Matt 13:30).

The names written in the Book of Life are those who believe Christ accepts the broken, the lonely, the confused, and the grieving who seek his compassion. "All that the Father gives me will come to me, and whoever comes to me I will never cast out," is the promise from Jesus (John 6:37).

Isaiah's voice is left to remind us: "In the time of my favor I will answer you, and in the day of salvation I will help you; I will keep you and will make you to be a covenant for the people; to restore the land and to reassign its desolate inheritances" (Isa 49:8).

Further Reading

Akwesasne Notes, ed. *Basic Call to Consciousness*. Rooseveltown, NY: Akwesasne Notes, 1986.

Barreiro, Jose, ed. *Indian Roots of American Democracy*. Ithaca, NY: Northeast Indian Quarterly, Cornell University Press, 1988.

Barreiro, Jose, and Carol Cornelius. *Knowledge of the Elders: The Iroquois Condolence Cane Tradition*. Ithaca, NY: Northeast Indian Quarterly, Cornell University Press, 1991.

Bonvillain, Nancy. *Hiawatha: Founder of the Iroquois Confederacy*. New York: Chelsea House, 1992.

Caduto, Michael J., and Joseph Bruchac. *Keepers of the Earth: Native American Stories and Environmental Activities for Children*. Golden, CO: Fulcrum, 1988.

Campisi, Jack, and Laurence M. Hauptman. *The Oneida Experience: Two Perspectives*. Syracuse, NY: Syracuse University Press, 1988.

Churchill, Ward M. *A Little Matter of Genocide*. San Francisco: City Lights, 1997.

Cornelius, Carol. *The Six Nations Series*. Ithaca, NY: American Indian Program, Cornell University Press, 1990.

Deloria, Vine, Jr. *Red Earth, White Lies: Native Americans and the Myth of Scientific Fact*. New York: Scribner, 1995.

Fenton, William, ed. *Parker on the Iroquois*. Syracuse, NY: Syracuse University Press, 1968.

George-Kanentiio, Douglas M. *Iroquois on Fire: A Voice From The Mohawk Nation*. Westport, CT: Praeger, 2006.

Grinde, Donald A., and Bruce E. Johansen. *Exemplar of Liberty: Native America and the Evolution of Democracy*. Los Angeles: American Indian Studies Center, University of California at Los Angeles, 1991.

———. *Ecocide of Native America: Environmental Destruction of Indian Lands and Peoples*. Santa Fe, NM: Clear Light, 1995.

"The Haudenosaunee Constitution." In *Traditional Teachings*, North American Indian Travelling College. Akwesasne, ON: North American Indian Travelling College, 1984.

Hauptman, Lawrence. *The Iroquois Struggle for Survival: World War II to Red Power*. Syracuse, NY: Syracuse University Press, 1986.

Jaimes, M. Annette, ed. *The State of Native America*. Boston: South End, 1992.

Jemison, G. Peter, and Anna M. Schein. *Treaty of Canandaigua, 1794*. Santa Fe, NM: Clear Light, 2000.

Jennings, Francis. *The Invasion of America: Indians, Colonialism and the Cant of Conquest*. New York: W. W. Norton, 1975.

FURTHER READING

Johansen, Bruce E. *Forgotten Founders: Benjamin Franklin, the Iroquois and the Rationale for the American Revolution.* Boston: The Harvard Common Press, 1982.

Johansen, Bruce E. *Life and Death in Mohawk Country.* Golden, CO: North American, 1993.

Keoke, Emory Dean, and Kay Marie Porterfield. *Encyclopedia Of American Indian Contributions to the World.* New York: Facts On File, 2002.

Loewen, James W. *Lies My Teacher Told Me: Everything Your American History Textbook Got Wrong.* New York: The New Press, 1995.

Lyons, Oren, and John Mohawk, eds. *Exiled in the Land of the Free: Democracy, Indian Nations, and the U.S. Constitution.* Santa Fe, NM: Clear Light, 1992.

McConnell, Jess. *Analysis of Documents Related to Residential Schools in Canada.* Saarbrücken: VDM Verlag, 2010.

McDonald, Thomas Michael. *The Black Book: Native Americans and the Christian Experience: Overcoming the Negative Impact of Nominal Christianity.* DTH diss., Carolina University of Theology, 2004.

Newcomb, Steven. *Pagans in the Promised Land: Decoding the Doctrine of Christian Discovery.* Golden, CO: Fulcrum, 2008.

Porter, Joy. *Land and Spirit in Native America.* Oxford: Praeger, 2012.

Porter, Tom Sakokwenionkwas. *And Grandma Said.* Bloomington, IN: Xlibris, 2008.

Slapin, Beverly, and Doris Seale. *Through Indian Eyes: The Native Experience in Books for Children.* Philadelphia: New Society, 1992.

Smith, Monique Gray. *Tilly: A Story of Hope and Resilience.* Winlaw, BC: Sono Nis, 2013.

Stannard, David E. *American Holocaust.* New York: Oxford University Press, 1992.

Swamp, Jake. *Giving Thanks: A Native American Good Morning Message.* New York: Lee & Low, 1995.

Stokes, John, and Dan Thompson. *Thanksgiving Address: Greetings to the Natural World.* Corrales, NM: The Tracking Project, 1993.

Tehanetorens [Ray Fadden]. *Wampum Belts of the Iroquois.* Summertown, TN: The Book Publishing Company, 1999.

Trigger, Bruce G., ed. *Northeast Handbook of North American Indians,* vol. 15. Washington, DC: Smithsonian Institution Press, 1978.

Venables, Robert W. *American Indian History: Five Centuries of Conflict and Coexistence.* 2 vols. Santa Fe, NM: Clear Light, 2004

Wagner, Sally Roesch. *Sisters in Spirit: Haudenosaunee (Iroquois) Influence on Early American Feminists.* Summertown, TN: Native Voices, The Book Publishing Company, 2001.

Wallace, Paul A. W. *The White Roots of Peace.* 1946. Santa Fe, NM: Clear Light, 1994.

Weatherford, Jack. *Indian Givers: How the Indians of the Americas Transformed the World.* New York: Crown, 1988.

Wright, Ronald. *Stolen Continents.* New York: Houghton Mifflin, 1992.

Some of these publications and others may be acquired from the following source:
Akwesasne Notes Book Store
Mohawk Nation at Akwesasne
PO Box 366
Hogansburg, NY 13655
(518) 358-3381
E-mail: administrator@mohawknation.org
Website: www.mohawknation.org

www.ingramcontent.com/pod-product-compliance
Lightning Source LLC
Chambersburg PA
CBHW031503160426
43195CB00010BB/1083